THE DEAD EYE BOY

BY ANGUS MacLACHLAN

★

★

DRAMATISTS
PLAY SERVICE
INC.

THE DEAD EYE BOY
Copyright © 2002, Angus MacLachlan

All Rights Reserved

CAUTION: Professionals and amateurs are hereby warned that performance of THE DEAD EYE BOY is subject to payment of a royalty. It is fully protected under the copyright laws of the United States of America, and of all countries covered by the International Copyright Union (including the Dominion of Canada and the rest of the British Commonwealth), and of all countries covered by the Pan-American Copyright Convention, the Universal Copyright Convention, the Berne Convention, and of all countries with which the United States has reciprocal copyright relations. All rights, including without limitation professional/amateur stage rights, motion picture, recitation, lecturing, public reading, radio broadcasting, television, video or sound recording, all other forms of mechanical, electronic and digital reproduction, transmission and distribution, such as CD, DVD, the Internet, private and file-sharing networks, information storage and retrieval systems, photocopying, and the rights of translation into foreign languages are strictly reserved. Particular emphasis is placed upon the matter of readings, permission for which must be secured from the Author's agent in writing.

The English language stock and amateur stage performance rights in the United States, its territories, possessions and Canada for THE DEAD EYE BOY are controlled exclusively by DRAMATISTS PLAY SERVICE, INC., 440 Park Avenue South, New York, NY 10016. No professional or nonprofessional performance of the Play may be given without obtaining in advance the written permission of DRAMATISTS PLAY SERVICE, INC., and paying the requisite fee.

Inquiries concerning all other rights should be addressed to The Gersh Agency, 41 Madison Avenue, 33rd Floor, New York, NY 10010. Attn: Peter Hagan.

SPECIAL NOTE

Anyone receiving permission to produce THE DEAD EYE BOY is required to give credit to the Author as sole and exclusive Author of the Play on the title page of all programs distributed in connection with performances of the Play and in all instances in which the title of the Play appears for purposes of advertising, publicizing or otherwise exploiting the Play and/or a production thereof. The name of the Author must appear on a separate line, in which no other name appears, immediately beneath the title and in size of type equal to 50% of the size of the largest, most prominent letter used for the title of the Play. No person, firm or entity may receive credit larger or more prominent than that accorded the Author. The following acknowledgments must appear on the title page in all programs distributed in connection with performances of the Play:

Originally Produced by
Cincinnati Playhouse in the Park
Edward Stern, Producing Artistic Director
Buzz Ward, Executive Director

New York Premiere at the MCC Theater, April 2001
Artistic Directors: Robert LuPone & Bernard Telsey
Associate Artistic Director: William Cantler

SPECIAL NOTE ON SONGS AND RECORDINGS

For performances of copyrighted songs, arrangements or recordings mentioned in this Play, the permission of the copyright owner(s) must be obtained. Other songs, arrangements or recordings may be substituted provided permission from the copyright owner(s) of such songs, arrangements or recordings is obtained; or songs, arrangements or recordings in the public domain may be substituted.

*To Jennifer
and Lily.
The light and love of my life.*

THE DEAD EYE BOY was originally produced by Cincinnati Playhouse in the Park (Edward Stern, Producing Artistic Director; Buzz Ward, Executive Director) in Cincinnati, Ohio, on March 18, 2000. It was directed by Charles Towers; the set design was by Karen TenEyck; the lighting design was by Nancy Schertler; the costume design was by David Zinn; the props were by Karla Knochelmann; the fight director was Drew Fracher; the stage manager was Emily F. McMullen; and the stage management intern was Victoria Hein. The cast was as follows:

SHIRLEY-DIANE .... Raye Lankford
BILLY .... Kyle Fabel
SOREN .... Dan McCabe

THE DEAD EYE BOY received its New York premiere at the MCC Theater (Robert LuPone and Bernard Telsey, Artistic Directors; William Cantler, Associate Artistic Director) on April 10, 2001. It was directed by Susan Fenichell; the set design was by Christine Jones; the lighting design was by Russell H. Champa; the costume design was by David Zinn; the fight director was Rick Sordelet; the production manager was Lester P. Grant; and the production stage manager was Stacy P. Hughes. The cast was as follows:

SHIRLEY-DIANE .... Lili Taylor
BILLY .... Joseph Murphy
SOREN .... Aaron Himelstein

CHARACTERS

SHIRLEY-DIANE, 29

BILLY, 32

SOREN, 14, Shirley's son

PLACE

North Carolina.

TIME

The present.

THE DEAD EYE BOY

ACT ONE

Scene 1

A family room in a rental house in the Piedmont of North Carolina. Painted-over plywood paneling, shag carpets of an indeterminate color. A living room area; couch and coffee table bought at This End Up — a kitchen door, two bedroom doors, and the front door. It is busy, messy, beaten up. But clean. Shirley, twenty-nine, is physically tiny with a rough voice that sounds like she was yelling all day yesterday — but it always sounds like that. Billy, thirty-two, looks forty-five — ruddy, dark complexion, bags under his eyes, muscle turned thick around his middle. They enter, falling through the front door, laughing so much they can hardly walk and talk. They may appear drunk, who can tell.

BILLY. Lord God deliver me.
SHIRLEY. I know, that's like —
BILLY. So funny — tell me — what she say? "Did you…?"
SHIRLEY. No, it — first — see — when she introduced herself — her —
BILLY. Yeah. Yeah.
SHIRLEY. Her — her —
BILLY. Name, yeah.
SHIRLEY. What?
BILLY. Name?
SHIRLEY. Name, right, name. Goddamn, I couldn't think of the word.

BILLY. And she ask you what?
SHIRLEY. Wait — what — which?
BILLY. This one. At tonight's meeting.
SHIRLEY. Oh she —
BILLY. "Are y'all bi-weekly?"
SHIRLEY. I know — S'what started me off. I couldn't —
BILLY. And you said what?
SHIRLEY. I said, "I didn't ever did such a thing in all my life." *(He guffaws.)* "Least not sober. Not that I can recall."
BILLY. That is some — some — some — *You* —
SHIRLEY. So then she introduced herself. *(He is convulsed.)*
BILLY. Stop.
SHIRLEY. And I thought she misspoke. I said, "Virginia?"
BILLY. "Virginia?"
SHIRLEY. And she said, "No. My name's *Vagina*, lady! Get it right!"
BILLY. No way. You lie.
SHIRLEY. That was a first, man.
BILLY. Vagina. What'd you say?
SHIRLEY. *(She turns to him.)* "Nice to meet you."
BILLY. Ohh.
SHIRLEY. *(Calming some.)* God. *(She goes to the kitchen. He gazes at her.)* You want fizzy?
BILLY. No, tap's good. Thank you.
SHIRLEY. Ain't that pitiful. All I can offer is water. *(She is heard offstage.)*
BILLY. Please, ma'am.
SHIRLEY. *(Offstage.)* Me too. I hate the fizzy crap. It's Soren's. You want ice in it? Or straight up?
BILLY. Yes, please.
SHIRLEY. *(Offstage.)* What?
BILLY. Rocks. Please.
SHIRLEY. *(Offstage.)* Right. *(She enters with two waters.)* What's all this please/ma'am shit?
BILLY. I'm being respectful.
SHIRLEY. Of what?
BILLY. You.
SHIRLEY. And you can kiss my ass.
BILLY. Gladly. *(She presents her ass.)*

SHIRLEY. Sir. *(He kisses it.)*
BILLY. How 'bout…? *(He feels her breasts.)*
SHIRLEY. Be my guest. Pay your respects. *(He nuzzles her.)*
BILLY. Marry me.
SHIRLEY. "My name's Vagina, lady!"
BILLY. I'm asking. Really. Shirley-Diane. Be my wife.
SHIRLEY. What?
BILLY. Will you?
SHIRLEY. What?
BILLY. Here it is. By summer I'm getting a new life, baby. I'm out of the factory. I mean it. I got plans.
SHIRLEY. Like what?
BILLY. Well, I been praying. Wait — And every time my Higher Power comes back at me with, "What's most important to you?" It ain't nothing I tried before. It ain't the drugs, or the service, or the drink, and it sure ain't the hole. None of that. It ain't even maybe money, or a good job — but — something I'm aiming for higher. And it come to me that that something might be — It's — now don't start.
SHIRLEY. I ain't saying a thing.
BILLY. You're fixing to crack up on me and this is tough — OK. Just — don't start looking like —
SHIRLEY. Like what?
BILLY. You know. Don't look at me.
SHIRLEY. Oh, come on.
BILLY. So — I go to the meeting last September and there you sit, all perky and. Pert.
SHIRLEY. Pert?
BILLY. You know. With your tits all — up, and all. Wait — And pretty soon we hook up and I start to think I, you know …
SHIRLEY. What?
BILLY. Feel. Something. I think. Wait — So I start asking myself, you know — "What the … hay's … going on?" And every time I ask myself, "What I want? What I want? What I want?', if I'm honest with myself — and that's what I'm aiming for, by God — If I'm honest, it comes back to one thing — and that's you. I'm pretty sure. *(She's suddenly very "sober.")*
SHIRLEY. — You got a ring? *(He hesitates.)*

9

BILLY. You can have this. *(He takes a large ring off his hand and gives it to her. It is enormous on her tiny finger.)*
SHIRLEY. I never seen that off your hand. Holy — Hell. Fuck. I just — I can't get over — I didn't know you were this serious a person.
BILLY. I'm serious.
SHIRLEY. Really?
BILLY. About this? I do believe. It's all new to me. But, I do believe. It feels true.
SHIRLEY. You thinking this all through the meeting tonight, all evening, or it just come over you?
BILLY. It's — I've been stewing it for a while. It's real, though, baby. It's really real. I may not deserve it, but I want a life with you.
SHIRLEY. Yeah. You're not that evil. What have you done to deserve me?
BILLY. That's not what I meant.
SHIRLEY. I'm not — Is it hot in here? Am I red?
BILLY. Let me see.
SHIRLEY. I feel all flushed. *(She giggles. He cups her crotch.)* Not there.
BILLY. No?
SHIRLEY. Not yet. But keep going.
BILLY. How's this? *(He rubs her. She closes her eyes.)*
SHIRLEY. Well, as the fella said — Ain't that a kick in the head.
BILLY. 'Sat good?
SHIRLEY. I never ever — I never thought this was going to go down when I brought you home tonight.
BILLY. This?
SHIRLEY. No. You know.
BILLY. I really mean it. Cross my heart and hope to die. What you say?
SHIRLEY. Oh — God — God — hold on. Go slower. *(He kisses her.)*
BILLY. OK. Let's take it slow. *(He takes a step back.)*
SHIRLEY. Nooo. I meant —
BILLY. Let's be grown-ups. OK? *(He offers her a cigarette.)*
SHIRLEY. Oh, hell yes. *(She takes a deep breath and takes a cigarette.)* I'd really like a good belt of something wicked.
BILLY. Baby. Don't even.

SHIRLEY. I'm kidding you! I'm just — Whew. *Is* it hot in here?
BILLY. My heart's 'bout busting through my shirt. Feel this. Feel.
SHIRLEY. How 'bout — can I feel it down here? *(She cups his crotch.)*
BILLY. Feel my blood pounding? *(She smiles, rubbing him. He responds. She speaks in a small voice, almost timidly — shaken.)*
SHIRLEY. You know it's crazy.
BILLY. Yep. It's scary to think this might be good.
SHIRLEY. It's a crazy idea. I'm out of my mind, you know.
BILLY. Yep. Why are we so messed up, can't just enjoy it?
SHIRLEY. Chronic relapser, fucked up.
BILLY. I know your tale. I heard it all. *(He sucks on her neck.)*
SHIRLEY. I got it all.
BILLY. I know you do.
SHIRLEY. I'll rip the heart out of you.
BILLY. Like hell.
SHIRLEY. I'll turn. You seen me.
BILLY. I know.
SHIRLEY. And I'm old.
BILLY. You're twenty-nine.
SHIRLEY. I feel old. Like, god, some old charred thing left after the house burned down.
BILLY. Aww. Baby.
SHIRLEY. God. And it scares me when people react to what you seem like. Sometimes at the car dealership, I'll be dealing with some complaint and I know I'm being a bitch and I'll see the person is scared of me and I get this odd feeling 'cause, um, like a part of me likes it. And then at the same time — I'm scared 'cause it's like — I feel like — it's real. I really am a snake.
BILLY. You're not.
SHIRLEY. Ugly, evil, old.
BILLY. You're beautiful.
SHIRLEY. Well, you're fucked up.
BILLY. This is true.
SHIRLEY. And you think you love me?
BILLY. Yep.
SHIRLEY. I'm supposed to believe you?
BILLY. Yes.

SHIRLEY. Huh. *(She pauses, breathing hard.)* You gonna move in here? Live with us?
BILLY. I thought.
SHIRLEY. Well. It's your funeral.
BILLY. Are you saying yes?
SHIRLEY. I guess.
BILLY. Really?
SHIRLEY. Yeah. I think.
BILLY. You want to think about it?
SHIRLEY. Nah, I don't want to think about it. Screw that. I say yes. Let's do it.
BILLY. Hell — well — Damn.
SHIRLEY. You cursed!
BILLY. I'll pay the money.
SHIRLEY. You *must* be excited.
BILLY. I'm like to pop. *(They both start laughing. They both become silent.)* I think I want to cry.
SHIRLEY. Ha! Pussy. *(She pauses.)* Me too.
BILLY. I hate this.
SHIRLEY. Me too. *(Soren, fourteen, and tiny to the point of seeming frail, comes banging in the front door with a large box. One of his eyes droops, considerably.)* What the — scared the shit out of me. *(Soren giggles.)* I thought you were in bed.
SOREN. Well think again. Oh. Look who the cat dragged in.
BILLY. Hey, Soren, what if we said we was getting married. What you think a that?
SOREN. You two?
BILLY. Yep.
SOREN. You want *her?* Saggy old bag of bones?
SHIRLEY. Up yours.
SOREN. Suck my dick.
BILLY. Whoa.
SHIRLEY. Somebody should slap that smartass grin off your face.
SOREN. *(Turns to Billy.)* You want to do it?
BILLY. Ahh.
SOREN. Daddy?
SHIRLEY. I'll do it. Any day. Any time. I knock you to kingdom come.

SOREN. Oh yeah? You and what army? I'll take you on. *(They slap at each other, giggling.)* Ain't got it in you.
SHIRLEY. I'll whip your ass. Come on. *(He smacks her hard.)* Hey!
SOREN. Come on. *(She smacks him hard back. They laugh.)*
BILLY. Goddamn. *(Shirley turns to Billy and smacks him.)*
SHIRLEY. You owe me more money! *(Soren joins in. They all tussle and laugh.)*
BILLY. I'd kill you both soon as look at you.
SOREN. Big man. Big talk.
SHIRLEY. Yeah. Daddy.
SOREN. Daddy?
BILLY. I'm not your — *(Shirley tickles Soren. On him.)*
SOREN. Stop — get off me. Get off me, bitch! *(She stops, smacks him, and gets up, slightly self-conscious, but not angry.)*
SHIRLEY. Go to bed.
SOREN. No. I got things to do. *(He takes his box and puts it on the table.)*
SHIRLEY. You got school tomorrow. Did you do any homework today?
BILLY. Let's you and me go on to bed. *(Shirley smiles at Billy.)*
SOREN. Yeah. *(Shirley turns to Soren.)*
SHIRLEY. You go soon. *(Soren gets a can of tuna fish and an opener, milk, and a small dish from the kitchen. Shirley turns quickly and begins to make out with Billy. Soren returns and opens the tuna.)*
BILLY. Good night, Soren.
SHIRLEY. Turn off the porch light.
SOREN. Hey, I don't want to hear her start howling again, like some old cat in heat.
SHIRLEY. Get used to it, boy. *(Shirley giggles and exits to the bedroom.)* And don't leave a mess. *(Billy exits to the bedroom. Soren puts the open tuna in the box. Billy returns, goes and gets glass of water from the kitchen.)*
BILLY. What you say? Think it's good?
SOREN. It's sick.
BILLY. It's good.
SOREN. What the hell difference does it make?
BILLY. Well. It'd be good if it was cool with you. *(Soren glances up at Billy. He takes in the glass.)*

SOREN. What's that for?
BILLY. My teeth. *(Soren smirks, but says nothing. He puts a saucer of milk in the box.)*
SOREN. Guess what I got.
BILLY. What are you now — thirteen?
SOREN. Close.
BILLY. Nah — fourteen.
SOREN. Chuck me that tape. *(He gestures to a roll of duct tape on the floor behind Billy.)*
BILLY. I wouldn't be fourteen again to save my life.
SOREN. Behind you.
BILLY. Not the way I — What — this? I woke up one time in a whole nuther city. In a whole different state, had no idea how I got there. Didn't have no pants on and found a dog licking my — Here — hey — heads! *(He hits Soren, accidentally, with the roll of duct tape. Soren turns on him — shocked. Then Soren moves on him with fists raised — eyes glaring.)*
SOREN. *(Fierce.)* Fucker. *(Billy instinctively puts his fists up. A moment of frightening, impending violence.)*
BILLY. Whoa. *(Then he checks himself, and "comes to.")* Hey — Sorry, boy, I didn't mean to hit you — *(Soren stops, and starts laughing.)*
SOREN. Right.
BILLY. Sorry. *(Soren goes back to the box, checking on what's inside.)* Not many come at me like that any more. You're lucky I didn't —
SOREN. I wish you would. *(Soren is straight-faced. Billy is confused. Finally Soren smiles — like it's a joke.)* Maybe someday. *(Billy laughs. Looks down — spilled water from his glass is on the floor.)*
BILLY. Shit — look at this.
SOREN. There's some paper towels in the —
BILLY. — Aww — and I cursed, too. Fuck. *(Billy rips off his shirt and wipes the water up. Soren stops and watches him, seemingly mesmerized.)* Don't tell her, she'll never know. *(Soren picks up the duct tape and goes to the box. He closes it, and starts taping it up.)* We'll get on. OK? I'm pretty easy to be around these days.
SOREN. And I'm a barrel of fun. *(Soren doesn't look at him, continues taping the box. Billy watches, thinking of the evening.)*
BILLY. I think this is good. I do.

SOREN. Could be. Time will tell. *(Soren looks at him.)*
BILLY. You say the damnedest shit, kid.
SOREN. You gonna pay me or Mom?
BILLY. Alright. We'll see you tomorrow. *(Soren looks up from the box.)*
SOREN. Promise?
BILLY. Huh?
SOREN. Tomorrow morning? You gonna be here? Forever?
BILLY. OK. Night ... *(Billy goes. Soren looks after him. Then he finishes sealing the box. There's a faint "Meww" from within it. Shirley and Billy are heard in the bedroom. Soren picks up the box and savagely throws it at the wall. He giggles. He hears Shirley giggling lasciviously from the bedroom.)*

Scene 2

Most of the stage is dark apart from an area where Billy sits in a folding chair. There is another chair beside him. He is hunched forward, in thought. When he speaks it is low. Shy.

BILLY. I got to say. Today I'm grateful. 'Cause. Um ... Well, I'll go ahead now. *(He sighs, and laughs a little, nervously.)* This morning at work. I got this boss, says we can't get off our machines till someone relieves us. But I — I says, enough of that, and went out back behind the building — just to have a smoke. *(Shirley enters noisily and sits in the other folding chair with two cups of coffee. She hands him one.)* Thanks, baby. So — I got this whole macho thing going on in my head — you know, I'm conducting this dialogue with myself: "You ... so-and-so," I say, "You're not a man letting him eat your ... " you know. And I'm confused and don't know what. And all of a sudden I look down, and right there at my feet was some pharmaceuticals, and works. In the dumpster. Right there at my feet. All wrapped up, pretty. *(He and Shirley laugh.)* Unbelievable. And — man — I mean to tell you. It was like Christmas.

SHIRLEY. Praise Jesus.
BILLY. Or Easter.
SHIRLEY. Umnph.
BILLY. My heart racing, I picked 'em up. I did. And I held 'em. A year ago? Six months ago? Olden times, I'd a'picked up a syringe on the road, rubbed it on a matchbook and used it no matter how dirty it was. And these were —
SHIRLEY. Oough.
BILLY. Like an answered prayer. At that moment. *(He pauses.)* It rocked me. What was it doing there? Why did I find it, at that minute when I was all — mixed up? But. Now. Here's the thing. Wait — I made a choice. By the grace of God I put 'em back. I put 'em down, y'all. I left 'em. *(He takes a deep breath. Shirley shakes her head slowly — doubtful whether she could have done the same.)* I hightailed it back inside, and I saw my boss and I gave him a big "Hello sir!" — big "blank"-eating grin on my face. And I went to my station and worked my behind off. All day. Like a real person. 'Cause, that's what I am now. A real person. And I'm here to tell you, I never thought I would be. Listen — I got normal problems. You know? *(He laughs with Shirley.)* I got a new wife — not that that's a problem. Honey. But I got a truck payment, and a teenager, and a boss that makes my butt walk barbed wire. I can't hardly believe it. I got a home. Y'all. A home. Now if that's not proof there is a God, I don't know what is. *(He stops a second.)* But I thought about that package in the dumpster all day. Don't think I didn't. Man … Here I am. And, when I think about where I come from.
SHIRLEY. Don't. *(He pauses again.)*
BILLY. And I do. I think about it. There's one thing I know, I ain't never going back in. Never. If I was faced with going back — I'd put a hot one through the roof of my mouth. Take myself out. And I've come close. I've heard that voice telling me to, often enough, so I know I could do it. *(He glances at Shirley.)* In the Marines, they teach you how, you know, t'scream real good. Real loud. And tear up somebody like a mother … 'scuse me, but, um, what they don't teach you is how to feel. Didn't no one teach me, ever, ever how. How to do nothing except be ugly. Mostly to myself. So when something came up. I couldn't handle it, I'd —

go off. You know. One way or other. Mask. But, since I been clean, um, I've acquired some feelings. Y'all know what I'm saying. I mean, I feel like a, some kind of alien, sometimes. I'm about a year old. I'm having to — I'm having to go against my nature here. Or, what I was shown. What I, what I, saw, coming along. Growing up. My past. *(He leans forward again.)* And it's a bitch. *(He turns to Shirley.)* I'll pay you the dollar. I don't know how the rest of the world gets through this shit without some ... something. 'Cause, you understand, I'm not saying everything's now all "One-Fifteen Rosy Street," you know. I'm not saying that. A lot of it's good but, you know — the dragon's still got you in its mouth, man. And you can think you got it down. That you've killed it. But — that's so much ... "stuff." It is. Illusion. 'Cause it's gonna rise up again. I know that. This is work, man. It requires constant vigilance. That voice is still there, lying in wait. Telling you it ain't worth it. Give up. Give in. Run for your life ... Pick it up. *(He takes a breath.)* I'm a rough tough guy, you know, but, it scares me, y'all. I'll say it. I know there's things I haven't faced yet. Inside me. Damn, I get sweaty just talking about it. *(He laughs.)* But — I'm changing the score. So help me God. I got hope. For, like, the first time I can recall. And it's 'cause of this program. And my Higher Power, and my family. *(He takes Shirley's hand.)* I got it all. And I'm holding on to this one, man. With both hands. Holding on and praying for grace. *(He laughs.)* Oh — if anyone's thinking 'bout buying a vacuum cleaner talk to me in 'bout three weeks, 'cause I may be able to help you out. That's all. Thanks for letting me share. I pass it to Shirley. *(He seems relieved and content. Shirley laughs, jovial.)*
SHIRLEY. I'm Shirley I'm an addict. *(She pauses while the group greets her.)* Well, I can't top Billy. But — let me see — since I've been clean I haven't fallen off a mountain. I haven't slapped any co-workers at Joseph Peebles Chrysler-Plymouth. I haven't gotten any diseases. I haven't sold my body or eaten out of the trash or even been arrested — although I'd like to kill my son, but that's another story. And, I just got me a good man ... to work around the house. Doing the odd jobs I can't get to, don't you know. So I'm pretty grateful myself. *(She laughs and glances at Billy. Softer.)* I'm awestruck, really. And just waiting for the other shoe to fall, as is my way. 'Cause, for some reason he loves me. One of those mys-

teries you got to just accept, I guess. Like grace. Don't ask too many questions and just move on. Oh — if any of y'all want to throw a prayer my way — my boy's fourteen now ... Need I say more? *(She turns to Billy, and they laugh.)* I'm happy there aren't any guns around the house. One of us would be in trouble. *(She sips her coffee.)* ... And ... what Billy was saying about the past. What I know is — there is no past for me. I buried that old life. I'm newborn, too. I made a decision — to not die, basically. And I left behind all the hell that happened to me. And that I caused. That old person — she's dead as far as I'm concerned ... I don't think about it, I don't talk about it, usually. What little I remember. 'Cause that just gives it power. And I been reincarnated. Really. And, let me tell you, y'all should be grateful 'cause you wouldn't have wanted to meet me in a dark alley ... Or — maybe you would. I don't know. All I know is I'm fucking grateful to survive and be here today and be clean. That's that. *(She laughs at herself.)* Thanks. *(They sit a moment, listening to others. They smile in unison at someone else's remark and Billy takes Shirley's hand and holds it, but Shirley drifts from her optimistic words to darker thoughts — memories that have been stirred. She furrows her brow, pissy. She turns to Billy and whispers.)* I swear this coffee is two days old ... I need a cigarette.
BILLY. I'm staying.
SHIRLEY. I'm gone.
BILLY. You OK? *(She gets up and tears out. Billy sits and leans forward, listening intently to the others.)*

Scene 3

Soren, nine years old now, stands over a spilled glass of milk, stunned. Shirley, twenty-three, stands across from him. Staring at him. She is very high, very drunk, swaying, and slurring her words. She speaks slowly.

SHIRLEY. What do you do? Think. *(He's silent. Looks at her, looks at the glass.)* Something spilled. Think. *(Soren looks at her. He takes his shirt off to mop.)* No! Not your shirt. Something spilled. Think. *(He's stymied. He puts his shirt back on.)* It's wet! *(He looks down at the shirt-tail — wet from the milk.)* God. You use a paper towel. *(He stares at her.)* Why do I even have to even tell you? *(He goes to the kitchen and comes back with a sponge and starts to use it on the floor.)* What are you — Don't use the sponge you clean the dishes with on the dirty floor. Think! Are you retarded? My God, Soren, are you a retard? *(She giggles.)* Do I need to take you to have your head examined? You're nine years old.
SOREN. Almost. *(Soren looks at the sponge in his hand.)*
SHIRLEY. Eight, nine. You're not a baby. Oh — get up. Do I have to show you? Do I have to take you by the hand? Do I have to show you how? Like you were a baby? Come here. Come on. *(She takes him and drags him in to the kitchen and stands in the doorway, pushing him in.)* Get it. *(He can be heard pulling the roll.)* Just a couple. Rewind it. You got to think of trees, Soren. You know, they have feelings, man. And when they, when we kill all the trees, there won't be no air. And you'll kill everyone on this planet. You want that? What's wrong with you? Now wet one. *One.* One. *(He is heard turning on the tap.)* You're splashing all over! Wipe that up now. *(He is heard pulling more paper towels.)* You know I got this job interview. You start this on purpose. You're doing this on purpose, aren't you? You're torturing me on purpose. *(She drags him back in the room. He trails a wad of paper towels.)* Come on. Grab up those others now you pulled them off the — Think of the trees!

Have some consideration for life, will you?! *(She jerks him by the arm back to the spill.)* Get down! *(She kneels down over him like two wrestlers ready for a match.)* What do you do now? *(He looks at her.)* SOREN! Use what God gave you! You're not a vegetable! You've got a brain. Use it. You're not an idiot. What's wrong with you? What is the matter! Goddamnit. Wipe it. *(She bends over him and wipes with him. They almost look like dogs humping — Shirley over him, on him.)* Get. It. All. I've got to show you how to wipe up a spill? I'm supposed to be there by — Fuck. I'm telling you — no more Nestle's Quick. Ever. Never again. Never! Ever! Ever, ever! Over there — get it all, or it'll be sticky and draw ants. You want that? You want to live with ants crawling in your bed? You'll fall asleep and they'll get in your ears and eat your eardrums, and crawl up in your head and eat your brain out. I had a friend that happened to — she was ... *(She pulls him up.)* Are you smiling at something I said? Goddamnit, I'll wring your fucking neck. What did I say? ... I was making sense, wasn't I? Come on. Fuck. What did I — Wasn't I? *(She jerks him around to face her, then she shrieks.)* Oh shit! Oh no. Goddamnit! You just got it on me! *(She throws the paper towels down and stands.)* There's a spot on my fucking skirt! I got a spot! There's a spot. I got a spot. Hand me that — I got nothing else sexy to wear! *(He tries to rub her skirt.)* Don't! Stop it. Why are you doing this? *(She bursts into tears.)* Why did I — I'm so stupid stupid! *(She grabs him and shakes him, over and over.)* Why do you hate me? You're a monster! *(She jumps up and down and cries like a child throwing a tantrum. She drops him on the floor and looks at him. She storms off. Soren sits looking after her, bewildered. Then he stands. And snickers, a little.)*

Scene 4

Most of the stage is dark apart from an area where Billy and Soren sit in the front seat of Billy's four-on-the-floor truck. Soren is behind the wheel. The motor is running.

SOREN. Can I please leave, please? I'm done. Can I please leave? *(Billy is silent.)* Why aren't you talking? *(Billy is silent.)* I'm not gonna get it. And you're gonna flip out on me any second, so I say forget the whole thing. Please.
BILLY. Did you want to do this?
SOREN. No. Not anymore. I'm getting out. *(They remain seated.)*
BILLY. If you want to take a time-out to think about it then that's fine, but not if you're just quitting 'cause you can't get it right off the bat. That's no way to be.
SOREN. It's a way for me to be. I'm too little.
BILLY. I was 'bout your size when I learned.
SOREN. I'm not you.
BILLY. By myself.
SOREN. Oh, big deal. You drive the getaway car, or what?
BILLY. You're not far off.
SOREN. ... Yeah? *(Billy looks at him, seeing his interest.)*
BILLY. I'm letting you sit in my new truck.
SOREN. Whoop-de-doo. *(Billy looks at him.)* You're not talking again? What are you looking at?
BILLY. Calm down ... You got a girlfriend? *(Soren laughs, embarrassed.)* What? Someone you like?
SOREN. God.
BILLY. Get your rocks off and enjoy it. *(Soren snorts.)* Find one who likes it. You got happiness. *(Soren is silent.)* Even just kisses.
SOREN. Let me out of here.
BILLY. Try it again. *(Soren turns away.)*
SOREN. Carla Renegar thinks I got "bedroom eyes."
BILLY. Huh? ... I didn't hear you. *(Billy touches his shoulder. Soren*

flinches.) ... OK, go on, put your foot on the clutch and the brake and put it in first.
SOREN. I can't do it. *(Billy looks at him.)* Stop looking at me.
BILLY. *(Gently.)* You make me laugh.
SOREN. Why?
BILLY. I don't know. I remember learning.
SOREN. ... How many times you been in jail? *(Billy looks at him.)*
BILLY. Too many. *(Soren looks at Billy. Billy continues to look back.)*
SOREN. Don't look at me and I'll do it. OK? Turn away. Turn away! *(Billy turns away.)*
BILLY. You want me to close my eyes, put my fingers in my ears? *(He does, and hums.)*
SOREN. You're really really cool, man. *(Billy smiles, stops humming and looks at Soren. Soren stares at him, and Billy turns away. Soren puts his feet on the pedals and struggles to put it in gear.)*
BILLY. Just a little gas, ease out —
SOREN. I know! Shush! *(He tries and stalls out.)* Fuck! *(Billy snorts a little, amused. Soren notices.)* What was that?
BILLY. Nothing. It just takes time. Everybody has trouble with it at first.
SOREN. I'm not going to do it! I can't get it! Can we go now, please? Come on. Why do you like this? You enjoy torturing me.
BILLY. Nah — *(Billy leans in to Soren. Soren flinches again.)* Look — *(Billy reaches over to show him something near the steering wheel and Soren springs and snaps at him.)* Hey! *(Billy jerks, instinctively makes a move to retaliate, and stops himself.)* Why'd you do that? *(Soren stares at him.)*
SOREN. ... I want to go! Do I have to engrave it on your head? Do I have — do I have to walk? *(Billy reaches over again.)*
BILLY. *(Calmly.)* I was going to show — *(Soren snaps again — biting Billy's finger. Billy pulls it back and stares at it.)* God — fuck. *(Soren glares at him. Billy looks at his finger.)*
SOREN. Get it? Reach over again I'll do it again.
BILLY. I can see the fucking bone. *(The finger is really bleeding. Billy gets napkins from the glove compartment and wraps it. Soren watches him for a reaction. Billy applies pressure to his finger, not looking at Soren.)*

SOREN. So. What are you going to do now? Huh? Beat my skull in? *(Billy concentrates on his finger, controlling his breath, suppressing.)*
BILLY. You need a muzzle.
SOREN. Why won't you do something? Say something to me! I don't know why you don't. *(Soren looks at him. Billy looks at Soren, no longer angry. Soren is holding and blinking back tears.)* Motherfucker. *(He turns the truck on, puts his feet on the pedals and puts it in gear. He tries easing it out, but the car heaves, moves a little, then stalls.)* Fuck me!
BILLY. OK — I think I better —
SOREN. You don't even tell me what to do right. I've driven before. It's this truck.
BILLY. OK, enough, I'm going to the Emergency Room. *(Soren turns to him, looking at Billy's hand, frightened.)*
SOREN. ... I'm, I'm sor — *(Then he looks at Billy and yells in his face.)* I could do it if you weren't here. Looking at me! I'm getting out and walking. And don't follow me, either.
BILLY. Go on, get out. *(Billy gets out of the truck. Soren watches him walk around the truck.)*
SOREN. You can have it. Shit. I don't care if I never get it. "Sit in your truck ... " "You got a girlfriend," what a bunch of doo-hockey. *(Billy opens the driver's side door.)*
BILLY. Get out.
SOREN. Drag me. *(Billy stares at him, amazed. He reaches in.)*
BILLY. You bite me you'll regret it. *(Billy takes Soren's arm and leads him out of the truck. Soren stands staring at Billy.)*
SOREN. What is your trip, man? What is it with you? You're not for real. *(Billy gets in behind the wheel. He closes the door.)*
BILLY. You want to ride with me?
SOREN. You're twisted! *(Billy puts it in gear.)*
BILLY. You coming? *(Soren stares at him.)*
SOREN. Don't follow me. *(Soren stands there. Billy pulls away [accomplished by the lights going down on him and the sound of the truck leaving]. Soren stands watching him go. Whispered.)* ... Don't come after me.

Scene 5

Shirley sits alone, talking softly, casually.

SHIRLEY. Thanks. Thanks. *(She giggles.)* That's all I can think of to — just — it's such a gift, god, I don't know what I've done — but — thank you. *(She takes a few breaths.)* Hmm. I've been thinking of Mr. Peebles. He needs help, man, really. He's been such a bastard to me. I know he hates women. I know he hates me. But I got to learn to keep my mouth shut around him so I don't lose this job, you know. So, if you could — I got to stop contradicting him in front of the customers. Even when he's completely fucking wrong and stupid and I know he'd make a better deal if he listened to me. — But I'm just the receptionist so — what do I know … But — if you could give him some wisdom. Or insight. You know? That would be good. And me a longer fuse. That would be really good. 'Cause — I don't want to blow it, you know — But he is such an asshole. *(She pauses.)* — Any of it. Umn. Can you — Can you — Um, just help me to believe in all this shit/stuff? More? Like … love. *(She giggles softly.)* You know. What Billy sees. You know? What my life could be. What it is, right now. All of it. 'Cause — you know how I am, man. I'll be going along OK, kind of wobbly but pretty good, and then — bam — it's gonna creep up out of the basement and come up on me. This — thing — in me. And I — I really — I just want to get rid of it. I do. Kill it. 'Cause it's a motherfucker. God. *(She stops.)* So, what do I do? God? When it comes on. The voice. The crap. It's so ugly, and weak and — familiar. So — familiar — How can I change it? What do I do? I — I just feel like I'm — I know I'm "powerless over people, places, and things" — I just — I need your help, OK? OK? Just — expand me. Expand my — heart. Tear it open. Go ahead. Just give me real strength — Not this Bitch crap but — real. 'Cause I'm — I'm so — I'm just so afraid … it's going to — Just — What I want is — make me better. You know? Keep me going. Keep the door closed. Keep the dead *dead. (She pauses. Softly.)* For Billy. God. For my man. Who loves me. *(She breaks down.)* Don't let anything fuck it up. *(She stops herself crying.)* I'm just ... scared I'm going to — That, you know, it's all just an illusion and he's really gonna get to know us and it won't be what he thinks we are and he won't like what he sees when he sees us, just like every other fucking man I ever brought — Fuck. *(She pauses.)* Make us clean. *(She stops.)* I'm so grateful, God. Thank you. I just want to believe in the good Shirley-Diane. The one he loves. That I don't even trust is there. 'Cause — God — I'm happy. *(She stops and laughs.)* Don't let any of us fuck it up. Anyone. Especially me. But. Anyone ... OK? OK? OK. OK, man. Over and out. I love you. *(She smiles, crosses herself like a Protestant who's seen it in movies, bops up and goes.)*

Scene 6

Billy fiddles with a vacuum cleaner in front of the couch, referring to a booklet from time to time and mouthing what he's read to himself — like rehearsing a part. He has a bandage on his finger. He turns on the vacuum. Behind him Shirley and Soren enter from the kitchen, tussling with her purse. It is not clear if they are playing or fighting. Billy, vacuum running, does not notice them. Shirley and Soren move back into the kitchen. Billy vacuums. Shirley and Soren re-emerge — still wrestling, in a tickling, full-body contact way. They both giggle.

SHIRLEY. No!
SOREN. Why? You got no good reason not to.
SHIRLEY. Yes I do.
SOREN. No you don't.
SHIRLEY. I say I do. *(They giggle.)*
SOREN. Why?
SHIRLEY. Because I say. I'm the adult here.

SOREN. Oh yeah? Prove it.
SHIRLEY. I am! Let go.
SOREN. I swear I won't do nothing bad.
SHIRLEY. You'll make me pee. Stop. Billy?
SOREN. "Billy?!"
BILLY. *(Not paying attention.)* Huh? *(Soren tickles her and she laughs, falling on the ground, Soren on top of her. He gets her purse and runs off into the kitchen.)*
SOREN. Ah-ha! *(She runs after him, laughing.)*
SHIRLEY. Son of a bitch! *(Billy turns off the vacuum, seeing her exit.)*
BILLY. What's going on? What are you doing? *(He waits — no response from other room. He pokes his head in the kitchen.)* What's the problem in here? *(They are both heard laughing and yell in unison: "Nothing!" and giggle. Billy returns to the couch and studies his instructions again, engrossed. Shirley enters with clean laundry to fold, followed by Soren. Both have a more "subdued" demeanor. She places the basket of clothes on a table and playfully thuds her purse beside it, looking back at Soren with a defiant twinkle.)*
SOREN. You don't play fair.
SHIRLEY. I'm not playing. Touch it and you're dead.
SOREN. It's not late. It's not bad. *(She turns her attention to her laundry. Soren glares at her, and makes a face behind her back. He looks over at Billy on the couch until Billy notices. Billy looks up at him.)*
BILLY. What? What do you want?
SOREN. I just —
SHIRLEY. He can't.
BILLY. Can't what?
SOREN. *(To Shirley.)* That's not what I was going to say.
SHIRLEY. Yeah, right.
SOREN. You don't know everything.
SHIRLEY. I do too. *(Soren laughs.)*
SOREN. Shut up. Billy?
BILLY. Don't talk like that.
SOREN. I need to —
SHIRLEY. Yeah, did you hear him?
SOREN. What?
BILLY. Shut up is disrespectful. Don't do that. What you need?

Come here. *(Soren glares at him.)* Come over here and sit down like a civilized person. Talk to me nice.
SOREN. Oh God. Give me a fucking break. *(He looks at Shirley. She smiles, amused. Soren smirks and shuffles over to the couch.)*
BILLY. What do you want? Just talk to me like you're a human being. *(Soren takes a big pillow on the couch and stuffs it in the front of his shirt.)*
SOREN. Um —
SHIRLEY. He can't. He's not one.
BILLY. He is too.
SOREN. Uh. No I'm not — *(He puts on a "stupid" voice.)* I'm a ape. I'm a pig. I'm, like, I'm an alien ...
BILLY. Come on, son. *(Soren imitates Frankenstein's monster. He picks up one of the vacuum's attachments as if it's a lit stick.)*
SOREN. Ohh fire! Fire no good. Noooo! *(Shirley guffaws.)*
BILLY. Hey — don't mess with my — *(Shirley keeps laughing. Soren throws it across the room.)* Hey! *(Soren throws another one.)*
SOREN. Bad! Bad! No like. Fire!
BILLY. Pick it up. *(Shirley still laughs.)*
SHIRLEY. Soren. *(She goes and picks up one of the attachments.)* Oh shit.
BILLY. Did he break it? *(Soren drops the "bit.")*
SOREN. I was just — *(Shirley's demeanor switches and she's angry.)*
SHIRLEY. This is coming out of your ass.
SOREN. Why you flippin on me? I didn't mean to.
SHIRLEY. Look what you did! You're always fucking around.
SOREN. I'm sorry, I was just — I was just — you know — I was just — *(He looks at Shirley. They catch each other's eyes and Shirley can't help herself — they giggle. Shirley stops.)*
SHIRLEY. Stop it! Don't make me — I'm mad.
SOREN. I didn't mean it. Really.
SHIRLEY. Tell him.
SOREN. *(To Billy.)* I'm sorry. I'll pay for it. Don't hit me. Master. *(Shirley, despite herself, snorts. Soren smiles, suppressing a laugh. Billy stares at the two of them, confused.)*
BILLY. ... What did you want — before — what was you going to ask me?
SOREN. I want to take my amps over to Corey's.

SHIRLEY. No one's taking you.
SOREN. I can drive myself.
SHIRLEY. You can not. You are such a fool.
SOREN. *(To Billy.)* Can I use the truck?
SHIRLEY. He's not taking you.
BILLY. It's late.
SOREN. Can I use it tomorrow?
BILLY. What do you mean use it? Not by yourself.
SOREN. Why not?
BILLY. You can't drive.
SOREN. He lives three streets away.
BILLY. It's illegal.
SOREN. Woo-ee.
SHIRLEY. He can't go at all. I don't like Corey. I told you.
SOREN. You don't know him.
SHIRLEY. I know him. And I know about that brother he lives with too.
SOREN. His brother's cool.
SHIRLEY. You can't go over there. That's it. *(Soren stills wears the pillow under his shirt.)*
SOREN. We just want to play music! *(Shirley folds her laundry.)* Fuck it! You say you want me to fucking do something with myself and then when I try to do something you don't let me do anything! Why don't you just fucking get rid of me. OK? And then you won't have to fuck with me anymore. It's all fucked up, and it's no fair at all.
SHIRLEY. Stop saying fuck. It's not nice.
SOREN. I tell you what — I'll just kill myself, OK? Save you the bother!
SHIRLEY. Would you? Please?
SOREN. Wouldn't it?!
BILLY. Hey.
SOREN. I'll just take a razor and slit my throat, OK? Or swallow Drano. That'd make you happy. Wouldn't it? I CAN'T STAND IT! *(Billy tosses his keys to Soren.)*
BILLY. Soren — heads! *(The keys hit Soren.)*
SOREN. Ow! WHAT ARE YOU DOING, MAN?! *(Soren and Shirley stop and look down. Soren sees the keys and grabs them.)*

BILLY. I'm sorry, I didn't mean to — Go on put your amp in the back of my truck, I'll take you tomorrow morning.
SHIRLEY. What?
BILLY. You playing music?
SOREN. Yeah.
SHIRLEY. *(To Billy.)* No you won't.
BILLY. That's it?
SOREN. That's it.
BILLY. Then I'll take you tomorrow.
SOREN. You will?
BILLY. Yeah. *(Soren looks at Shirley, then turns back to Billy. Soren smiles.)*
SOREN. Oh I get it. *(He turns back to Billy.)* — Is this like — "New Daddy gives Baby candy so he'll smile"?
BILLY. Huh?
SHIRLEY. I said no. *(Shirley snatches the keys out of Soren's hands.)* I said you can't go over there. I forbid it.
SOREN. You can't "forbid" me.
SHIRLEY. You better just shut your mouth.
SOREN. I'll do what I want. And he said I could go!
SHIRLEY. I said you couldn't. *(She turns back to her laundry, away from him. She thwaps the keys down on the table in front of her. Soren turns to Billy.)*
SOREN. So now what? Can I go? Or what? *(Billy hushes him and mouths "Don't worry about it.")* Tell me! You gonna let her get away with that? 'Cause this sucks! You hear me? I don't — I don't — I don't LIKE THIS! *(Shirley turns on a CD very loud — maybe Lucinda Williams — to drown him out.*)* ONE BIT! *(Soren goes up behind her and makes his hand into a "gun" and "shoots" her. She doesn't notice.)*
BILLY. Come here. *(He pulls Soren to the couch and tells him that he'll drive him tomorrow if he wants, if he'll just calm down. Soren argues back, Billy tells him it's cool. Shirley folds her laundry at the table. Soren protests, and stuffs another pillow under his shirt. Billy assures him. Soren considers, then seems to calm down. They look at Shirley's back — still folding laundry and singing along. Billy asks Soren to pick up the other attachment he threw. Soren looks at him,*

---

* See Special Note on Songs and Recordings on copyright page.

debating. Then he goes and gets the attachment. He hands it to Billy. Billy smiles at him. Soren smiles back weakly, sickly, slightly mocking. He goes to his room and slams the door. Shirley hears the door slam. She turns up the music even louder, defiantly, then turns it down some.)
SHIRLEY. Asshole. *(Billy goes up to Shirley and puts his arms around her, from behind.)* Get off of me. *(She doesn't push him away.)* I don't want him there.
BILLY. You say no, he'll do it anyway. You know that. *(Billy rubs himself close to her. She lifts her head back to his, they kiss. She turns to him and kisses him ravishingly. They move over to the couch and she gets on his lap. They start to make out, Shirley on top of him. Billy stops and looks at Soren's door.)*
SHIRLEY. He locked it.
BILLY. You sure?
SHIRLEY. Who gives a fuck. *(Shirley pushes him on his back and starts to undress him, getting off on the "danger." Billy undoes her shirt, feels her breasts. She takes his shirt and puts it in his mouth like a gag. He takes it out, laughing, and ties it around her eyes like a blindfold, as she rubs herself on his crotch. They kiss some more, too involved to notice Soren's door has opened and he watches them. Soren comes out of his room, the pillows still under his shirt. He creeps, expertly, to the table and picks up the truck keys. Billy and Shirley are too heated to pay any attention, the music still plays. Soren goes by the back of the couch and makes his hands into a gun and mocks shooting them both. He opens the front door and they pay no notice. He exits, then almost immediately comes back in, taking the pillows from out of his shirt, he throws them across the room. Shirley, still blindfolded, hears the muffled thud and turns her head in that direction. Soren is gone.)* What was that?
BILLY. Nothing. *(She stops and takes off the blindfold. She sees the pillows. Billy's truck is heard cranking up outside, and with some clutch-popping, it is heard peeling off.)*
SHIRLEY. Hey.
BILLY. What?
SHIRLEY. He's stealing your truck.
BILLY. He — what? He can't drive. He can't — *(Shirley runs out the door, screaming.)*
SHIRLEY. *(Offstage.)* Soren! Goddamn you! *(Shirley is heard*

screaming after the truck, Billy runs out.)
BILLY. *(Offstage.)* Holy — Shit. *(They are heard arguing.)*
SHIRLEY. The fucker took my car last fall.
BILLY. What?
SHIRLEY. Last fall! This time, though — man — I've had it with him!
BILLY. When? *(Shirley storms back in. Billy follows.)*
SHIRLEY. I swear. I'm at the end of my — goddamn — leash! *(She turns off the CD.)*
BILLY. He did it before?
SHIRLEY. Are you deaf?
BILLY. Don't do that. Just tell me. He took your car?
SHIRLEY. Yes. YES!
BILLY. How long for? How long was he gone that time?
SHIRLEY. What am I going to do with him? I — I'm — he's out of control!
BILLY. Come on, let's go, Shirley. Let's take your car and go look for him.
SHIRLEY. No.
BILLY. Why not?
SHIRLEY. I'm calling the cops.
BILLY. What?
SHIRLEY. I've had enough.
BILLY. Wait, now —
SHIRLEY. I want him arrested ... I do. *(She goes to the phone and dials 911.)*
BILLY. Hold on a minute — Shirley —
SHIRLEY. Last fall it was two days, he was gone two days and I had no fucking idea where — *(On the phone.)* Yes. I need to report a crime. Oh. OK. *(To Billy.)* Till I found him with that Corey kid and his fucking dealer-brother.
BILLY. What?
SHIRLEY. You heard me!
BILLY. We'll go there. Come on!
SHIRLEY. And what? Ground him? No, I was too chicken-shit to go through with it last time but this time he took your truck and by god he's going to jail.
BILLY. No. *(He cuts off the phone.)*

31

SHIRLEY. Billy!
BILLY. Think. You don't want to do that. He's fourteen.
SHIRLEY. He just stole your truck, Billy.
BILLY. I know that.
SHIRLEY. We're pressing charges.
BILLY. No we're not.
SHIRLEY. I am!
BILLY. It's my truck. And we're not. Did he come back last time on his own?
SHIRLEY. I don't want him back.
BILLY. Think where he's at, Shirley. Don't you remember being that age?
SHIRLEY. No. I don't.
BILLY. Well, I was in jail when I was fifteen, and it didn't stop me from doing jack.
SHIRLEY. It got you out of the house.
BILLY. It just made me madder.
SHIRLEY. You don't know this boy, Billy.
BILLY. And meaner. And smarter about stuff I had no business knowing.
SHIRLEY. You just don't get it. You're stupid.
BILLY. What.
SHIRLEY. Ignorant, I mean. That's what I meant to say. Of this boy. 'Cause — he wants — he wants to fucking waste what's between you and me. *(Billy stops.)*
BILLY. Uhn-uh.
SHIRLEY. He's thinks he's going to do it to me again.
BILLY. He's not.
SHIRLEY. You're damn right he's not. 'Cause I'm not messing around anymore.
BILLY. I don't think that's so. Shirley.
SHIRLEY. You don't. Well, guess what else. He's on it, Billy.
BILLY. What do you mean?
SHIRLEY. This morning I found crack in his room. *(Billy stops, stunned.)*
BILLY. Oh … jeez —
SHIRLEY. Triple A, right-on shit. *(Billy stares at her.)* Yep. In my house.

BILLY. Our house.
SHIRLEY. And I found it.
BILLY. Oh, baby. What did you do?
SHIRLEY. ... I flushed it.
BILLY. Good, baby.
SHIRLEY. It nearly killed me.
BILLY. Don't call the cops. *(She collapses on a chair.)*
SHIRLEY. *(Quietly.)* ... If he was a rat, with a disease, we'd put out poison in the basement ... He's bringing it home. I can't — I can't stand — I can't — I'm doing what's right. I'm going to get him out of here. And it'll show him what happens in the real world ... Little son of a bitch.
BILLY. Don't call him that.
SHIRLEY. He is!
BILLY. It don't come out — It doesn't sound good.
SHIRLEY. He's a fucking son of a bitch! Why shouldn't I say it?
BILLY. 'Cause — That makes you the bitch. *(She slaps him. Then, she realizes.)*
SHIRLEY. Oh. I got it. *(She giggles.)* Come here. *(He moves to her. She collapses in his arms.)* I hate him. I hate him. *(He quiets her.)*
BILLY. Let's go look for him. *(They start kissing again.)*
SHIRLEY. *(Quietly.)* ... Do you love me?
BILLY. Umhn. I do.
SHIRLEY. I love you so much. *(She kisses him with desperation, holding on to him. He responds, enraptured.)* ... Would you do anything for me?
BILLY. Uhmn-huh. *(She becomes very sexually aggressive with him, pushing him down to the couch.)*
SHIRLEY. *(Softly.)* I just want — I want you to —
BILLY. Tell me.
SHIRLEY. ... Forget it. *(She pins his arms under him, and slugging, and slapping, and tickling, and kissing him. He gets very hot.)*
BILLY. *(Murmuring.)* Oh god. I want my fat cock in you. Baby. *(They start to make love.)*

Scene 7

Most of the stage is dark apart from an area where a ten-year-old Soren sits beside Shirley. They are in a Counselor's office. Soren slumps in his chair and displays no signs of anger or unhappiness, except that he slowly tears up a small composition book to tiny shreds throughout the session. Shirley tries hard to be attentive and concerned but she is completely high. She thinks no one can tell. Shirley looks over at Soren, quietly focused on ripping up the notebook.

SHIRLEY. Do you want to? *(He doesn't respond.)* I'd like to, um, read it. If you want. *(He glances at her and smiles. She smiles, they tend to make each other laugh. Shirley turns, out front, to the Counselor.)* I'm sorry, Dr. Treadway — he gives me these looks. *(Soren giggles. She tries to suppress hers.)* It's terrible. We'll be in church — when we go — which is not often, but we try — there's a lot of reasons why we don't, I know — but Sundays, you know, if I've got one day — that's it. He leaves me alone, the phone doesn't ring. And if I've been out ... Anyway — what was I saying...? Oh, yeah — he's a little devil, 'cause he knows, all's he has to do is look at me cross-eyed and I piss. Excuse my words, my language — wet myself — I don't know why, it's just something we have, I guess. He did it as a baby. *(She pauses.)* I don't mean he wet himself. He makes *me* — But — he did do that, you know, too — *(Soren is giggling. She joins him.)* He even now — you know, at night — he pees the bed. Wets in the bed. And he's ten. Right?
SOREN. Nine and —
SHIRLEY. I had to get one of those plastic sheets from my girlfriend whose kids pee, I mean wet, so much they ruined the mattress. Like cats. 'Cause cats, when they pee something — you can't get that out. Ever. Ruins. Whatever. Whoo-boy ... I'm sorry. I'll stop now. *(She finishes laughing.)* So. *(To Soren.)* What do you have?
SOREN. I'll be ten in two months.

SHIRLEY. Big deal. *(Mocking him.)* "I'll be twenty-four in three months." That makes us even.
SOREN. Hardly. You're old. *(He smiles at her. She smiles back.)*
SHIRLEY. Dr. Treadway says you wrote something.
SOREN. Yeah. Maybe.
SHIRLEY. A story?
SOREN. Yeah.
SHIRLEY. What's it about?
SOREN. Stuff.
SHIRLEY. Stuff. Sounds great. *(He giggles at her ribbing.)* You want me to read it?
SOREN. I guess. If you want.
SHIRLEY. I don't care. He thinks I should. If you don't want me to —
SOREN. OK. *(She waits.)*
SHIRLEY. You gonna give it to me?
SOREN. If you want.
SHIRLEY. I want it. Let me see. *(He slowly reaches under his chair and gives her a folded up piece of paper.)* Is it good? Will I like it? Is it funny? *(Reads.)* "Rough Life, my story by Soren Horace Watts." *(She glances at him. Lightly mocking.)* Ohhh. *(He smiles. She smiles.)* "Once there was a kid named Soren Horace. His mother was Shirley-Diane Watts. She got raped at the age of fourteen by some body, who knows who?" *(She takes a small pause, but doesn't look up, and keeps reading.)* "That's how she got pregnant with Soren. The kid blamed hisself 'cause she would have forgot if he never was alive. When I look in the mirror I see the Dead Eye Boy. The reason his eye was like that is 'cause his mom got raped and what happened in childbirth. That's what looks back at me when I see myself. What will happen to the Dead Eye Boy I don't know. But he won't be around for long, that's for sure. The end." *(Shirley stares at the paper. Soren keeps ripping up the composition book slowly.)* It should be himself. Hisself isn't a word. *(She looks at the Counselor.)* Right? *(She waits.)* Is that what you think? *(Soren doesn't say anything.)* Is it? *(She waits.)* Is that, like, what you're telling me here? *(Referring to him tearing up the notebook.)* Like, why you're doing that there? *(She waits.)* When I told you all that I was messed up, I shouldn't — I didn't mean for you ... Listen, what happened to

me was my business and it doesn't have anything to do with you. You know — I think of it, like, it happened to another person even. *(He shrugs his shoulders.)* It's dead and buried and forgotten. So it's nothing for you to worry about. *(She pauses — fighting away something deep. And managing to. He doesn't look at her.)* And, if you wasn't wanted. Well, hell — um — I mean — You know about abortions? You know what they are. You're smart. Do you think that wasn't an option? I could have. My mother — But, I didn't. 'Cause I thought ... Or — god — Don't you know about adoption? ... *You* know. *(He doesn't speak.)* I kept you 'cause I wanted you 'cause I loved you you were mine. You were somebody for *me* to have. You were mine to keep. *(She waits.)* I made a decision. At that time. *(She turns out towards the Counselor.)* Trying to make something good to come out of something bad. *(Pause.)* You know? I was raped. I was fourteen. *(Pause.)* It was my choice. I thought. Back then ... Then I forgot all about it ... That's it. *(She shakes her head.)* Anyway, he knows the truth. *(He finishes tearing up the notebook and throws the last piece to the ground. He turns and stares at her. She doesn't, and won't, look at him.)*

ACT TWO

Scene 8

Soren enters carrying a box. He puts it on a pile of other boxes. He carefully arranges them. He takes a chair and sits, facing the door. There is a hammer on the table. He idly picks it up and fiddles with it, and hums. Billy enters with groceries, stops, and stares at Soren.

SOREN. Hey. Did she flip out? *(Billy stares at him.)* I'm back.
BILLY. Where's my truck?
SOREN. It's not — nothing happened to it. It's in back. I washed it, even.
BILLY. Your Momma's behind me. You got your story?
SOREN. It set her off? Was she worried? Did she say anything?
BILLY. Where'd you go?
SOREN. Nowhere. Just around. I just had to get out. I'm sorry.
BILLY. She wanted to call the cops. *(Pause.)* You hear that?
SOREN. Yes sir. I brought your stuff in. The stuff in the boot of the truck. Look — all your stuff is in, now. This is everything, I checked. So — you're all moved in now.
BILLY. OK.
SOREN. I detailed the inside too. With a hose, you know, vacuumed it all out, and all. Not that it was bad — 'cause, it's new, but — it's real clean, now.
BILLY. Un-huh.
SOREN. Full tank.
BILLY. Umm. *(Pause.)* Let me tell you something for your own good. May I?
SOREN. Sure.
BILLY. Next time you need to get off, you tell me. And then go.

Just say you need to get away, and tell me like — how long, you think. That's all. But if you got it in mind to take my truck or your Momma's car, or any car that doesn't belong to you, I swear I won't be able to stop her from siccin' the law on you. And I'll tell you — you do not want to go to prison. Even county. You do not want that.
SOREN. Yes sir.
BILLY. That's not a threat, that's real.
SOREN. Yes sir. I'm really really sorry. I am. I won't — I know it's wrong. I won't do it again. It was stupid — it was a dumb thing — So. What do you think she'll — *(Shirley enters with groceries.)*
SHIRLEY. Did you not hear me say I needed your help? *(Billy runs to take a bag from her.)*
BILLY. I didn't hear you, babe. *(She sees Soren and stops.)*
SOREN. Hey.
SHIRLEY. Are you alright?
SOREN. I'm sorry.
SHIRLEY. Are you?
SOREN. It was really bad, and I won't ever do it again. I'm sorry. I'm really sorry.
SHIRLEY. You are so lucky.
SOREN. Why?
SHIRLEY. Billy said you'd turn up.
SOREN. Um — I was messed up. I was disturbed, Momma.
SHIRLEY. Uh-huh.
SOREN. Bad.
SHIRLEY. Where'd you go?
SOREN. Nowhere.
SHIRLEY. What did you do?
SOREN. Just rode around.
SHIRLEY. Yeah?
SOREN. I — I —
SHIRLEY. Were you with Corey?
SOREN. Nah. I was off by myself.
SHIRLEY. Are you lying to me?
SOREN. No, ma'am. I'm really sorry.
SHIRLEY. Did you get high?
SOREN. No. No, ma'am.
SHIRLEY. Did you steal money from my purse?

SOREN. No, ma'am.
SHIRLEY. You didn't.
SOREN. No. I won't do anything like this again.
SHIRLEY. You won't?
SOREN. No.
SHIRLEY. That's your word?
SOREN. I thought about what I did, and I know it was bad to worry you and take Billy's truck and be gone last night and all but I had to — I was all mixed up, you know, with school and classes and everything and this girl — Sheri — who dumped me for Carl Corday and all and I wanted to play music and you forbid me and I knew I was gonna explode on somebody and that wouldn't be good, so instead of hurting anybody else I just ran away from it all and drove around and I was upset and really mad and that's it and — I came back. No big deal. *(Shirley goes to him. He looks up at her. The hammer still in his hand.)*
SHIRLEY. No big deal.
SOREN. Nah. *(She slaps him really hard. The hammer goes flying out of his hand.)*
BILLY. Shirley.
SOREN. I came back. *(Soren is near tears.)*
SHIRLEY. No big deal.
SOREN. I came back.
SHIRLEY. You do it again, don't come back.
BILLY. He said he won't do it again.
SHIRLEY. What?
BILLY. He knows. OK? *(She scoffs, snorts.)*
SHIRLEY. Oh. Right.
BILLY. Huh?
SHIRLEY. You're a part of this family. You should take your belt off and do something.
BILLY. Do what? Think that'd teach him something?
SHIRLEY. He'd remember if it hurt.
BILLY. We talked about it. He understands what's what.
SHIRLEY. He's playing. He's bullshitting.
BILLY. Now, wait —
SHIRLEY. Nothing gets through to him.
BILLY. The boy says he won't do nothing like this again and we

ought to trust that.
SHIRLEY. You are such an idiot.
BILLY. Shirley. Don't speak to me like that.
SHIRLEY. You are, man. You're blind.
BILLY. I take the boy at his word till he proves me wrong.
SHIRLEY. Well, stick around, 'cause you got your head up your ass, and you'll find out I'm right. I'm so tired of this.
BILLY. You speak civilly or not at all to me.
SHIRLEY. I'll say any damn thing I want in my own house.
BILLY. Not to me. I won't take that.
SHIRLEY. Ha!
BILLY. There's no call for — I'm telling you —
SHIRLEY. Fuck you, man. *(She turns on Soren, who is smiling, slightly.)* I can still press charges, you know. You committed grand larceny. It doesn't matter that you brought it back, you did it. I'm still trying to decide. You remember Odell Renigar?
SOREN. Uh —
SHIRLEY. That's what he was in prison for — grand larceny — for ten years. And they fucked him in the ass and he got AIDS and died. Sound like fun? *(Soren tries hard to suppress a smile.)*
SOREN. No. Ma'am.
BILLY. You don't teach him anything by threats. *(Shirley sees Soren's smirk. With Soren looking at her Shirley has to work hard from cracking up as well.)*
SHIRLEY. You want to be slapped, don't you?
SOREN. Yes ma'am. No ma'am.
BILLY. OK, Shirley, you got milk here.
SHIRLEY. I know what I got. You can put it away as easy as me. *(She stands over Soren, still in the chair.)* Don't think you're gonna get away with it. *(She stares at him, intensely. He starts to cry.)* This is my life I'm fighting for. The one I built. Steal a car, or money from me again and you're gone. *(She grabs his face.)* So help me God, you won't break me ... And whatever you do from now on ... all I can do is pray for you ... But, if I ever find crack in my house again I'm locking the door against you. Yesterday morning I felt strong. Today I feel strong. I don't know about tomorrow. So, I don't care who you are — if you keep using you're just another addict to me. And I will do everything in my power to get you out

of my life. (*She moves away from him and takes an enormous breath, fighting back the weight of her emotion, wiping her eyes.*) I'm not having it. (*She turns, utterly exhausted, and moves to Billy and the groceries.*) Which bag is melting? (*She picks up a bag and takes it in the kitchen. Soren is crying. Billy slowly moves a bit to him. Soren has his head lowered.*)
BILLY. It's real. I'm sorry, but — it's the real … stuff. (*Soren has his head lowered. Shirley comes back and gets another bag.*) I'll be in to help you in a sec. (*When Shirley speaks it is now without emotion — the beginning of one of her "affectless" downward spirals.*)
SHIRLEY. (*Without antipathy.*) Whatever. (*She goes in the kitchen. Billy moves cautiously to Soren.*)
BILLY. If it scares you, that's good. It should. 'Cause — it should. (*Soren nods, slightly.*)
SOREN. I'm shit. (*His head shakes. Billy goes to him and puts a hand on Soren's shoulder. Soren flinches, but he lets the hand stay. His body shakes.*) She wants me dead. (*Billy stands by him. He squeezes his shoulder.*)
BILLY. … Hey, thanks for bringing my things in. (*Soren slowly lifts his head a bit, but doesn't look up at Billy.*)
SOREN. Your old stuff.
BILLY. Yeah.
SOREN. Books and things.
BILLY. My whole life. Yeah. You look through it?
SOREN. Nah.
BILLY. If there's some book you want, just ask. (*Soren looks up at Billy, he is no longer crying.*)
SOREN. She won't let you keep it. There's no room. She doesn't like clutter.
BILLY. Huh?
SOREN. You'd do better to throw it away. Before she does.
BILLY. Well.
SOREN. Smells like a basement.
BILLY. Oh, it's probably got some mildew on it. The books, and things. (*Soren smells his hands.*)
SOREN. It's gross. (*Soren smiles oddly at Billy. He gets up and picks up a bag of groceries as Shirley comes out of the kitchen.*) I'll help.
SHIRLEY. You're no help.

SOREN. Am too.
SHIRLEY. Am not.
SOREN. Am too. *(They both go in the kitchen with groceries. Billy goes to his boxes. He picks up a book and smells it. It stinks of mildew. Shirley and Soren are heard, faintly, giggling in the kitchen.)*

Scene 9

Most of the stage is dark apart from an area where Billy stands with the vacuum cleaner, attachments, a clipboard, and pots and pans. He is dressed in an uncomfortable looking coat and tie. To overcome his shyness he is being consciously "bright."

BILLY. ... I'm excited to be here! Can you tell? Because Rainbrite has been in business for over sixty years and we have just two goals in mind — building a product that gives good service for years to come. And, the second is having products that will make our homes a nicer place to live. Isn't that exciting? I think so. Can you tell? *(He clears his throat.)* OK, now — this is really great — Here's — *(He holds up a brochure.)* A free gift! I'd like to give you. Three days two nights to your dream destination — what's your dream? The beach or the mountains? Now, I'm writing today's date and I'm signing it for your dream to come true. Right now. And, that's good for one year. *(He writes.)* I get all excited. OK. *(He checks his clipboard and looks around and picks up a frying pan.)* OK. I want you to feel how heavy this pan is. *(He holds it out.)* Quality cookware is heavy. Now, that's a pan you could really do some damage with. Plus — all our Rainbrite cookware stacks, cooks like a dream, is easy to clean, and even stores easy. *(He sets it down.)* You could win our six piece deluxe set just by providing us with four qualified leads in fourteen days. Isn't that unbelievable! What I'd like is for you, while I set up my Rainbrite vacuum, is to jot down the names of as many people you can think that'd help you earn a set of this cookware. *(He drags the vacuum cleaner over, with attachments.)* Just, um, — if you think of anyone during my demo — you just keep jotting 'em down. *(He pulls the vacuum closer and catches his breath.)* We only need three things to live — air, water, and food. Everything else — we can do without really. Really. But we need 'em clean. Air, water, and food. Sometimes, in our homes, we think it's clean but — have you ever seen sunlight come in and seen all the dust particles blowing in the air? You think you're breathing clean — living a good life, but it's there. You can barely see it, but that can make you sick, with allergies and runny noses and such. But we can take control of our lives. We can! Good health is a matter of choice. The Rainbrite not only vacuums — it cleans the air, too! And, with this attachment — it can "Aromatize" with Four Fragrances — Pine, Lemon, Rose, and Rainbrite: "the smell after a shower." *(He smiles.)* I'm pumped. Now. I got a penny. *(He digs in his pockets for the coin.)* Here ... *(He digs in other pockets.)* Shoot. *(He can't find it. He laughs, nervously.)* Do you happen to have a — Wait — there — I knew I had one. OK. Do you think your cleaner could pick up a penny? *(He tosses the coin on the floor. He turns on the machine. He runs over it. It takes a few times, but does suck it — rattling on its way. He yells over the motor.)* Is that something? *(He holds the end out — it's deafening.)* That'll suck anything you got, man. *(He laughs. He turns it off and speaks "intimately.")* Now, I'm going to do something unheard of. I'm going to offer to leave you this machine, uh, with you overnight, so you can try it yourself. Because I trust you. I do. And I'm so sure that if you were to use this yourself you'd be just as excited about Rainbrite as I am. *(He takes a breath, and speaks "confidently.")* OK. My job's finished. I came out for two reasons. First reason, to bring you a nice gift and get to know you people, and second, to show you the Rainbrite. They tell me if you are interested, you'll let me know. *(He smiles and takes a step back. He speaks quickly.)* It's been an exciting pleasure to spend time with your family today. Oh — I'm going to leave you with one last thing. We call this our Opportunity Knocking Brochure. Because I hope you might consider some part-time or full-time work and become a member of the Rainbrite family, same as me. Because it's the very best thing that ever happened to me in my life. I mean it. *(He waits, smiling.)* Ever. *(His face and energy drops.)* Aw, crap. *(He sighs.)* I go over it and over it — I do it for my wife, and I — I — believe it, Vonda. I believe in Rainbrite. I know I believe what I'm saying. Oh! I didn't mention dust mites — shoot. I keep forgetting that. I did try and, tried to keep it light, you know. Like you said. I tried to be more personable. Was I? Personable? Should I get up more dirt, you think? Talk more about the importance of clean living? — I think maybe — take more time to show how powerful it is? *(He turns on the machine and cleans.)* Like — *(Vonda stops him. He turns it off and takes a deep breath. He tries to remain optimistic.)* You're the boss, Vonda — any suggestions you got — I'm just, I'm dying for 'em. *(He waits.)* Hey, did I tell you I gave notice at the plant? ... Go ahead. Shoot ... I just got to make that first sale. It's coming, though. Anyday. *(He mocks himself, lightly.)* ... I'm excited. Can you tell?

Scene 10

Billy moves slowly to the table studying the want ads, silent and worried. He sits. The table is set for dinner. Soren shuffles out of his room and glumly plops himself down at the table with a box and a leather bag, a roll of duct tape, and a hammer. He rummages through the box and selects one or two small, hard plastic toys to go in the leather bag. He puts them in, then takes the hammer and smashes them in the bag. Billy glances at the action, but goes back to his paper. Silence.

SOREN. ... You know who I really hate? Tyler Basley. *(Billy doesn't respond. It doesn't seem to matter to Soren. He puts more plastic figures and toys in the bag.)* ... And Corey *really* hates him ... Mike Coulter and I, we go, "OK, we'll beat him up for you tomorrow," since he wasn't going to be in school — 'cause of Corey's suspension ... And Corey is like, "No. Tell Tyler Basley I want him dead! And scream it in his face!" Real intense. Really angry. Freaky ... We're like, "OK Corey" ... Then I say, "If we tell him that, you

know how much trouble you'll be in? Since you had that gun with you at school?" ... Then Corey was like, "Yeah, I know. Forget it." *(He starts sealing the bag with the duct tape.)* ... But I still wanted to do something to Tyler Basley ... 'Cause I hate him. *(He smashes the toys in the bag. Billy doesn't respond.)* Corey was just showing off with that piece ... You had guns, right? *(Billy reads the paper.)* You did stuff like that. ... He's not gonna pop anybody. *(Billy doesn't respond.)* I bet you have. *(Soren starts smashing the bag with the hammer. Off and on.)* Or, even hurt someone bad ... *(The sound bothers Billy.)*
BILLY. What are you doing?
SOREN. Getting rid of some stuff. You mind? *(Billy looks at him, then goes back to the paper. Soren keeps staring at Billy.)* So — how does it feel to take somebody's life?
BILLY. What?
SOREN. You'd probably feel bad afterwards, but I don't know what it would be like at the time. I bet there'd be some feel of some kind of power. *(He pounds some more.)* ... Not like I want to kill anybody, you know. I'm just asking — you know — like a philosophical discussion.
BILLY. Put this ... all this away, supper's ready.
SOREN. Momma ran over our cat when I was little. It was an old cat. It was mean. She was all upset, but I was glad ... I guess when it's you who did it it's harder to laugh at. Maybe. *(He smashes the bag with the hammer.)* And cats aren't people.
BILLY. Stop it! *(Soren laughs.)* Now.
SOREN. It's a gas. *(He smashes some more.)* You want to? *(Billy violently grabs the hammer away from him and throws it to the floor.)*
BILLY. Not today.
SOREN. What's up with you? *(Billy goes back to the paper. Whispered.)* Jerk. *(Billy ignores him.)* It wasn't against the law.
BILLY. I said stop it.
SOREN. Killing a cat. You couldn't go to jail for it. Give me that back.
BILLY. What?
SOREN. My hammer. *(Billy glares at him a second.)* Break my arm, next time, OK?
BILLY. Did you bring that slip for us to sign?

SOREN. It's in my bag.
BILLY. How long you got to stay after?
SOREN. Through Friday. It's such crap. I sit there in that room — I was thinking about killing myself I was so pissed off.
BILLY. Umn.
SOREN. I thought about using my shoelaces.
BILLY. Doesn't work. Get the slip and I'll sign it.
SOREN. I'll get it later.
BILLY. Get it now.
SOREN. I can't wait till I get my license, man. I'll run over dogs, squirrels, little kids ...
BILLY. Oh yeah, that sounds good. That's really cool.
SOREN. Is it? *(Billy turns and looks at him.)*
BILLY. I never killed anyone.
SOREN. Can I go to Corey's after dinner?
BILLY. Your Momma said no.
SOREN. What do you say? *(Billy looks at him a moment.)*
BILLY. Another night. *(He looks at his paper.)*
SOREN. No.
BILLY. I'm not taking you.
SOREN. You'll do what I say.
BILLY. Huh? *(He looks at Soren.)*
SOREN. Someday. *(Not antagonistically.)* So — why is everybody in a mood? ... What's wrong with you? *(Billy tries to ignore him.)* ... Dad. *(Billy looks at him, trying to determine if he's being jerked around. Billy sighs.)*
BILLY. Aww. I got a fucking ... Excuse my — *(He stops himself because of the curse word.)*
SOREN. I don't give a shit. *(Billy looks at Soren again, then decides to proceed.)*
BILLY. My supervisor — Been riding me.
SOREN. Yeah? 'Cause he knows you're quitting?
BILLY. I guess. ... So, we got all this new equipment in — so I was working on this new piece, and he comes up — stands there and watches me — and instead of helping me he says "You're not getting it," and he — he — man, he comes up and pushes me aside.
SOREN. What did you do?

BILLY. Whew.
SOREN. D'you deck him?
BILLY. I came this close, man. This close.
SOREN. Oh, man, you should have.
BILLY. He didn't know.
SOREN. I would have. Someone lays hands on me ... That's what a man does.
BILLY. I held it in, I held on. I started praying for serenity.
SOREN. Fuck that.
BILLY. I was asking my Higher Power — give me strength.
SOREN. Pussy. *(Billy turns on Soren, then controls himself.)*
BILLY. No, it was the right thing to do.
SOREN. Liar.
BILLY. What.
SOREN. You were just scared.
BILLY. ... You don't know how it is, son.
SOREN. I know a pussy-move. I'm not your son.
BILLY. Let me tell you something —
SOREN. I don't shirk. I take care of things.
BILLY. No one calls me a liar.
SOREN. You wanted to smash his face. If you don't face the truth you're a liar. Right?
BILLY. You apologize to me.
SOREN. Make me.
BILLY. Right now.
SOREN. I dare you.
BILLY. Soren. *(Shirley comes in with food. She has dark circles under her eyes and seems smaller — depressed. Billy looks at her. Soren also notices her demeanor.)* You OK? *(Her voice is low.)*
SHIRLEY. Macaroni and cheese, and I don't want to hear any yucks.
SOREN. Yuck.
BILLY. *(To Soren.)* Hey.
SOREN. I'm teasing. I love macaroni and cheese. Especially Momma's. *(She sits, and starts to eat, dully.)*
BILLY. *(To Shirley.)* What's up? *(She shrugs.)*
SHIRLEY. Maybe I'm getting something.
SOREN. I love it burnt.

BILLY. Soren.
SOREN. I'm serious! We always eat it like this. It's good. *(Soren tries to catch Shirley's eye to make her laugh but she doesn't look at him. Billy steals glances at Shirley, concerned.)*
BILLY. I'm thinking of putting the truck up for sale, Shirley.
SOREN. What?
BILLY. We got to do something. I mean, that payment every month. We can use it.
SOREN. Don't sell it!
BILLY. I'm not going to have it coming in right away, so much. So, it's an idea. You think I ought'a — what d'you think, babe?
SHIRLEY. I don't know.
SOREN. No. We need a truck. I'm going to need it. Come on, man. Don't. It's the only reason we keep you around here. *(Soren shoves Billy, playfully.)*
BILLY. Back off! *(Shirley snaps to — angry.)*
SHIRLEY. *(To Billy.)* What's wrong with you?
SOREN. I was playing.
BILLY. He's trying me.
SHIRLEY. You don't have to bark. *(Soren jumps up, upset.)*
SOREN. I'm out of here! *(Shirley grabs his shirt and pulls him back to his seat.)*
SHIRLEY. Sit the fuck down and eat! *(She rips his shirt.)*
SOREN. You bitch! *(He grabs her by the neck. Without thinking Billy jumps up and pulls Soren away.)*
BILLY. You never. Never touch her like that. *(Soren stands, staring at him, amazed, and a bit thrilled.)* Sit down and eat. *(Soren sits. Shirley glowers at Billy, furious. Billy sits and eats.)*
SHIRLEY. *(To Billy.)* I don't want you to "protect" me. *(Billy turns to her.)* I don't need you to fight my fights. *(Soren smiles. Shirley turns to him. Ugly.)* You little shit. Why are you even … you make me sick. *(Billy looks at Shirley, taken aback at the venom. Soren's collar is ruffled and she reaches over to fix it. She now speaks with no anger at all.)* Your collar's up — *(Soren grabs her hand, and snaps at her, trying to bite her. Billy jumps up, grabs Soren's hand, grabs the roll of duct tape, pulls Soren from his chair and tapes his hands behind his back. He pushes Soren back into his chair and shoves his head down towards his plate.)*

BILLY. Now eat. *(He looks at Shirley.)* Eat. *(He sits. He starts to eat.)* I like it burnt some myself. It's good. *(Soren glares at Billy. He glances at Shirley. Shirley doesn't look at him. She sinks into herself and picks at her food. Billy eats. Shirley turns to Billy as if she's going to say something, but with no anger or animosity — with no affect at all. She stops herself and turns back to her meal. Soren smiles slightly. Shirley has the faint traces of a smile.)*

Scene 11

Most of the stage is dark apart from a lit area where Billy sits in a folding chair. There is another, empty, folding chair beside him. He's keyed up and halting.

BILLY. My name is Billy, I'm an addict ... I don't know if this is exactly related to drugs, but. Well I ... I'm losing my. A part of me is. I'm out of a job. Last day at the factory was Friday. But — things are going alright ... *(He stops himself from covering.)* Well ... It's a little rough. *(He pauses. Then speaks slowly.)* Hell ... The dream came back. Some of y'all may have heard it before. But ... In it I'm young. Just driving, just started. And I'm high. I feel great. It's a great high. Warm. The "bubble." But. I'm driving down the highway and I lose control and I hit another car — and it bursts into flame. Then I see this man rush out of the other car, screaming. And he — he runs around trying to open the other door 'cause. 'Cause his baby's in the back seat. And the car's burning ... I get really scared, then. Really rocked. I'm just a kid, and I've messed up, you know. Bad. I panic. And I leave. So they don't know who hit 'em ... But as I'm flying away I see in the rearview the man pulling a black thing from the car. And I see it move. It's his baby. Burnt. Black. Like coal. But still alive ... Then it's later. The baby lived. I see it. But it doesn't have no face, or hands. Just — its face is a mask. Like, scar tissue and eyes. Screaming from the pain, and growing up ... And the only form of power the — the boy — has as he's going through all the pain — is his voice — the only thing that gets through — is when he's screaming — to his father, or crying. Pleading, "Please be gentle. Please be gentle." ... And I know. I did this ... *(He pauses again.)* He's pushing me for something he wants. They threw him out of school, he's testing everybody. He's acting out. Drugs ... I know it — exactly. *(He pauses.)* I want to hit him. I see him, I think about the anger I felt at his age. It's like looking at myself and I'm so angry with him. He makes me feel like I'm ... I'm my dad. I want to beat the hell out of him. He's driving his mother — ... — Oh, she's got a little cold. She didn't feel up to coming tonight. *(He stops himself again.)* ... Well, she's at loose ends ... We're scrambling, y'all. I'm out of one job. And not bringing anything in. We got rent, and insurance, you know. It's a tough time. *(He stops.)* Tough time. Temptations. *(He can't go on, and consciously "covers" with some optimism.)* ... We'll be OK, though. Thanks for letting me share. *(He finishes and leans forward, ready to listen to someone else. One knee bounces, though, and he's still preoccupied.)*

Scene 12

Loud music — Lucinda Williams? — plays on the CD player.* A vacuum cleaner is heard offstage. The door to Soren's bedroom is open. Shirley emerges from Soren's, vacuuming. She is giddy and high, but it may appear, at first, that she is just in a light-hearted mood. She dances, sings, and vacuums. Soren enters with a backpack over his shoulder, a tool kit, a roll of duct tape, and an empty Coke bottle, chewing gum.

SHIRLEY. Hey, baby. You have a good time? *(He doesn't respond.)* No answer. *(She vacuums over near him and tries to dance with him. He moves away, annoyed, and puts his things on the table, but leaves his backpack on. She giggles. He picks up the Coke bottle and things,*

---

* See Special Note on Songs and Recordings on copyright page.

studying them, figuring out how to put them together for some device. Shirley vacuums up to him again and rubs herself on him, singing.)
SOREN. You sound like shit. *(He can't suppress a giggle.)* Get off. What's with you? *(He looks at her. She glitters at him. He looks at his room — the door open. He runs in his room. She stops a second, considering, a worried look over her face. Then she sings along with the CD some more, putting it out of her mind. Soren runs back in the room.)* You bitch! *(She laughs.)*
SHIRLEY. You're smart.
SOREN. That's my stuff! *(He shoves her. She smiles and shoves him back.)*
SHIRLEY. So?
SOREN. You got no right to go in my room and go through my things!
SHIRLEY. Says who?
SOREN. It's mine!
SHIRLEY. I was cleaning. *(She laughs and vacuums over to his door.)* How much it run? 'Cause it's good, boy. Where you get the cash? From my purse again?
SOREN. No!
SHIRLEY. I don't mind. You wanna share? *(She gestures with her head for him to join her in his room.)*
SOREN. You fucking crazy — god — wait till Billy finds out. *(She laughs.)* Why?
SHIRLEY. What?
SOREN. You were doing good.
SHIRLEY. Oh. Fuck it.
SOREN. Momma. You were doing good.
SHIRLEY. It's all … good, now. *(She leaves the vacuum cleaner, still running, by the door, and slips in his room.)*
SOREN. Get out of my room! Get out of there! *(He runs in after her. He is heard yelling at her. There is the sound of a scuffle. Shirley is heard laughing. Shirley runs out of his room, laughing, and running her finger along her gums.)*
SHIRLEY. You're — selfish. *(Soren runs out after her, screaming at her.)*
SOREN. I'm serious — shit! *(He knocks over the vacuum cleaner — which makes it even louder. Soren grabs her and jerks her around.)*

You stupid, stupid bitch! *(She laughs. He shoves her down on to the couch and crouches/kneels on top of her.)* Stop it. You've really screwed up, do you know that?
SHIRLEY. Come on, don't be a poot.
SOREN. Do you know what you've done? Do you realize what you've done? *(She stops for a second, seemingly "sober.")*
SHIRLEY. I know.
SOREN. No you don't! Think! *(He draws back his hand like he's going to slap/hit her.)* Do I have to? To get through to you? Do I? *(She smacks him, hard. He grabs her and they wrestle. She begins screaming.)*
SHIRLEY. Stop it! Stop! You're hurting — *(He covers her mouth and hits her.)*
SOREN. I hate you! *(He is on top of her. Billy enters from the front door, annoyed at the loud music and vacuum cleaner. Shirley screams. Billy sees them on the floor. He races to them and pulls Soren off her. Soren slings his backpack off and starts beating Billy with it.)* It's her! She — she's the one. She's done it again! *(Shirley gets up and begins to hit Soren.)*
SHIRLEY. Stop it! Stop it, Soren!
BILLY. What's going on! What are you doing? *(Soren throws his backpack at Billy.)*
SOREN. Get away from me! I'll kill you both.
SHIRLEY. Son of a bitch! *(Soren turns again to Shirley and slugs her.)*
SOREN. Bitch! *(Billy throws Soren to the floor. Soren tries to hit Billy, and starts biting.)* It's her! She's fucked it! I'll kill you both! I swear! *(Billy throws him on his stomach and sits on him. Soren flails. He's surprisingly strong.)* Get off! Motherfucker! I'll blow your fucking head off. *(He wriggles over towards his backpack — reaching. He grabs it and starts to dig in it, desperately — a gun? Shirley grabs the duct tape and gets behind Billy and grabs Soren's wrists, and with Billy's help, they tape Soren's hands behind him.)* Liars! You're both liars! You're dead! YOU'RE DEAD! I'll do it!
BILLY. Enough of that. Enough! *(Soren thrashes around and bites Billy.)*
SOREN. I got you. *(Billy pulls away to look at the bite. Soren turns and looks at Billy. He laughs.)*
BILLY. Shut the fuck up. *(Billy hauls off and really slugs Soren,*

sending him across the floor.)
SHIRLEY. Billy! *(Concerned, she runs to Soren, who is still conscious. She reaches down to him.)* You OK — ? *(Soren bites her hand.)* Shit! He bit me! *(She turns to Billy. Soren does, too.)*
SOREN. OK, Daddy. OK. Daddy. Come on. I'm ready. *(Infuriated, panicked, Billy grabs the duct tape and tears off a piece and wraps it around Soren's head, over his mouth.)*
BILLY. There. *(Billy pushes him face down again — hands tied, mouth covered. Billy leans on him, holding him down. He takes a breath and "recovers" himself. To Shirley.)* My god. What the hell's going on? *(Shirley, still frenzied, picks up the duct tape and rips it from the roll. She begins to wrap more tape around Soren's head, over his mouth — round and round. More and more.)* Shirley. What the fuck happened? *(She keeps wrapping. Soren struggles.)* He's not going anywhere. *(Soren thrashes wildly.)* We got him, OK? Stop it! *(To Soren.)* Settle down. You're not going anywhere. *(Billy uses all his weight to stop Soren, sitting on him, Soren face down. Soren keeps trying to move. To Shirley.)* That's enough! *(She stops taping Soren's head. Soren keeps thrashing, trying to make a sound, shaking and dipping his head.)* Shirley? Why was he on you — tell me — *(He looks at her and she glitters back at him. Her anger is gone. She smiles at him, and giggles.)*
SHIRLEY. We were playing.
BILLY. *(Stunned.)* What — ? *(Soren tries to get up, desperately. Billy stays on him, but is focused on Shirley. Shirley gets up and goes and turns off the CD and the vacuum cleaner. It is quiet. Billy stares at Shirley, incredulous. Soren stops moving.)* What did you do? *(Soren tries one more thrashing. Billy stays on him. Soren stops and lies still. Billy watches Shirley. She goes over to the table and picks up the Coke bottle.)*
SHIRLEY. I think this is a bomb. He was making. *(Billy gets up and goes to her. Soren doesn't move.)*
BILLY. *(He grabs her and looks in her eyes. Quietly.)* Babe. What did you do? *(Shirley looks sober.)*
SHIRLEY. Nothing new. *(She glances at Soren, motionless on the floor.)* He wants us dead. *(Shirley strolls back into Soren's bedroom. Billy turns to look at Soren on the floor. Soren isn't moving at all. The color drains from Billy's face. The lights come down except a spot on Billy and a spot on Soren, inert on the floor.)*

Scene 13

Shirley enters the front door, dressed up. She is at the end of a high but merely seems composed, and in a good mood. She slings off her shoes.

SHIRLEY. Ohhh. God. *(She laughs. Billy follows, in suit and tie, not laughing.)* Glad that's over. *(Billy goes to the couch and sits, loosening his tie. Worn expression, Shirley hikes up her dress.)* Look at this! *(The crotch of her pantyhose has worked itself way down to almost mid-thigh. Shirley laughs again.)* The whole day — these are the worst! *(She starts to yank them all the way down and off.)* I couldn't hike 'em up, I didn't think. Not in front of everybody. It was pitiful. Help me. Pull. *(She sits beside him and gets him to help pull the feet. She loses her balance and laughs.)* Wait! *(They get them off.)*
BILLY. I got to —
SHIRLEY. Whoo. That's better. I was suffocating. Now I can get some circulation going. Get some air up there.
BILLY. Shirley. *(She straddles him.)*
SHIRLEY. Our health teacher used to tell us you got to, or you get yeasty. You were looking mighty handsome in your suit, though. Did I tell you? *(She starts to kiss his neck.)*
BILLY. I got to decide ...
SHIRLEY. You know what I was doing?
BILLY. ... Something.
SHIRLEY. I kept pretending like it was our real wedding. A fancy-schmancy "do," you know. Everybody dressed, looking nice. *(Her kisses bother him and he pulls back a bit.)* I couldn't have stood it, otherwise. *(He pulls back some more. She stops and looks at him.)* Did you see that Detective Hennesee? In the back. And that policeman, and the butch lady from Social Services, they came too.
BILLY. Stop.
SHIRLEY. Ballsy. Considering it was their fucking fault we had to wait till almost Memorial Day to have a service. I think every

addict we know was there too. That was sweet. It really touched my heart.
BILLY. It was nice. Of them.
SHIRLEY. We never got a party, Billy. It was like a nice wedding reception. Without crappy punch. *(She kisses him tenderly.)*
BILLY. Shirley!
SHIRLEY. What? Don't you want to fuck?
BILLY. What are you thinking of?
SHIRLEY. Sucking your dick, baby. *(She smiles, flirtatiously. He looks at her. Delicately.)* It's a month. You haven't fucked me in over a month.
BILLY. Holy — smoke. You're —
SHIRLEY. What? *(He looks at her.)* What are you looking at? *(He continues to stare at her.)* Oh come on. God in heaven.
BILLY. Yeah.
SHIRLEY. Yeah. Exactly. And when I pray over it my Higher Power gives me peace. And tells me I got a lot to be thankful for.
BILLY. Like what?
SHIRLEY. Like how it turned out for us. Like we're not in jail, baby. You know? Like it could have been a whole lot worse. With your record. But by the grace of God the truth came out, for a change.
BILLY. The truth.
SHIRLEY. Yes. *(She pushes his face away.)* Come on! Stop looking at me.
BILLY. I'm not saying —
SHIRLEY. Stop it! I got stuff to do. *(She starts to get off him. He holds on to her.)* Let go.
BILLY. Wait a second.
SHIRLEY. Let me up. I want to take this dress off.
BILLY. Shirley, what should we do?
SHIRLEY. You're pissing me off now.
BILLY. Don't leave me. Come back. Come on.
SHIRLEY. I'm not going anywhere.
BILLY. I think I — maybe I should. Go back to the police. Or something. *(She stops struggling and looks at him.)*
SHIRLEY. What?
BILLY. To ... I don't know.

SHIRLEY. No! What you think that would do? And say what? We went through it all. It's all over. It's passed. Why are you torturing me with it? It was an accident and nobody's to blame. You can't eat yourself up with it. You got to go on. It doesn't do any good to look back. I just give it up to God and I go on.
BILLY. This is — this is — you can't just go on.
SHIRLEY. You have to.
BILLY. You can't.
SHIRLEY. I can. *(He looks at her a second or two.)*
BILLY. But you can come back, too.
SHIRLEY. Fuck you.
BILLY. Just decide to face it.
SHIRLEY. I am. The way I know how. Asshole. *(He takes a breath.)*
BILLY. Where do you think he is now?
SHIRLEY. Who? *(He looks at her.)* Jesus, Billy.
BILLY. I love you.
SHIRLEY. You think so?
BILLY. Yes.
SHIRLEY. Really?
BILLY. Yes. You're all I got. You're everything. I don't want to lose you.
SHIRLEY. Then fuck me! That's what I need.
BILLY. We — I — I think — Shirley. Listen. Wait. That was wrong. 'Cause. I. I. When it happened. It was an accident but I could have. I wanted him ... I. Just at that moment, I ...
SHIRLEY. Shut up! Let me go!
BILLY. You did too. *(He starts to cry, losing control. She tears herself away.)*
SHIRLEY. How can you say that? He was my fucking — !
BILLY. I know!
SHIRLEY. You're out of your fucking mind, man.
BILLY. Wait!
SHIRLEY. Get a grip.
BILLY. My — my — I can't. I don't know what to do. I don't know how to think. I don't know — how to — how to — deal. I got to tell someone. I got to tell.
SHIRLEY. Grow up. *(She turns and moves towards Soren's room.)*

BILLY. Don't go in there. *(He grabs her.)*
SHIRLEY. I have things to do.
BILLY. All we got to do is look at it. That's all we can do. It would be so much easier to not ... But it doesn't work. You can't numb it.
SHIRLEY. Shut up.
BILLY. I want to — Me too! — I want to close my eyes but he won't let me.
SHIRLEY. Shut up.
BILLY. I want to go back like before and not feel anything but he's watching me now. In my dreams. Burnt black. I carry him. I'm carrying him around. He's still pleading with me.
SHIRLEY. Let it go! Don't talk about it.
BILLY. We'll always have this. We can't bury it!
SHIRLEY. We just did.
BILLY. It'll kill us! ... Do you understand what I'm saying? Something's not finished. *(She stops and comes to him.)*
SHIRLEY. *(Calmly.)* Do you believe in a power greater than yourself?
BILLY. ... Yes.
SHIRLEY. You don't act like it. It's a loving, compassionate God. You believe that? ... He has some reason for this. He has some reason for taking my ... — For the whole thing. There's a reason behind it. Everything. My whole fucking life ... We can't second guess him. It's a mystery. We've just got to take it on faith. We can't figure it out. It's too much for ... Too much for ... *(She cracks, and starts to cry.)*
BILLY. I just — I think I just — I want him to know. I want to tell the boy something. *(She shakes her head, wanting to object, speak, but can't get any words out.)* I wish somebody could have told him when he was ... — that it was OK. I wish somebody could have took away his fear.
SHIRLEY. Ahh.
BILLY. And give him. A feeling. I never. No one ever.
SHIRLEY. Stop. Please.
BILLY. Gave me.
SHIRLEY. I couldn't...! — Stop. I got to go —
BILLY. Please, God. Let him know. Let him know. *(He breaks completely. She runs in to Soren's room.)* I love him. *(Shirley is heard rum-*

maging around offstage. After a few seconds her voice is heard, struggling to come back under control.)
SHIRLEY. *(Offstage.)* Your ex-boss-lady from Rainbrite came up to me. *(She is heard stopping. Offstage.)* She was saying nice stuff about you. I said, "Then why the hell did you fire him?" You never told me she was so fat. *(She giggles from the other room. Then there is silence. Offstage.)* Umm. You want food? We got some casseroles left. I don't — I'm not going to be hungry. *(She comes back in with a plastic storage container of toys and a box, wiping her nose. She puts the boxes on the table and stuffs one box with the contents of the second. They are Soren's items. She gets a bloom of energy, and laughs. Billy stares at her. She fills the box.)* I knew this girl, once, who worked for the airlines and she and her husband used Smucker's jam — played with it, you know — up her diddlewad. And then — they ate it, swear to God. *(She rips off some duct tape and seals the box.)* When I was little I ate dirt and pennies. *(He turns and stares at the sound of the duct tape.)* It didn't hurt me. I drank creek water that I know was polluted, but I never got sick. I think it makes you more resistant. I never get sick. *(She drops the box on the floor and goes back to the door to Soren's room.)* There's a lot of shit to clean up. *(She turns and looks at him, light shifting, glittering, from her eyes.)* You could — uh — Come do it with me. It would be good. For you. *(She slides into Soren's room. There is silence. Billy stands up, looking towards the room. Then she's heard offstage again.)* I need the help. You know, love. ... Come on. *(Silence.)* 'Cause. Lord knows — it'll take me an eternity to get through this. He had more crap ... Come on in, love. *(She is heard humming some. Billy turns away, agonizing.)* So — Billy? What do you think about that story? ... About the jam? Billy? *(She laughs.)* Don't get any ideas. Hah! Too messy. *(He goes to the door to Soren's room. She hums. He stands by the door. Wavering over going in, or not. She hums. He turns and goes out the front door, leaving it open.)* In your dreams, maybe ... *(Billy reappears in the front doorway, reaches in, and quietly closes the door.)*

Scene 14

The stage is dark. Slowly a tight spot of light comes up on Billy sleeping on the ground, dreaming. His shoes are off and placed nearby. He takes a deep breath. Then a tight spot of light comes up on an area where Soren stands by a spilled glass, at a loss. He looks at the glass. He looks around. Billy sees Soren and turns to him. Billy stands.

SOREN. *(Softly, to himself.)* What do I do? ... Think ... Think. *(Soren, panicked, looks at the glass and takes his shirt off, crouches down but hesitates. He looks up at Billy. Billy takes off his shirt and goes to Soren. He kneels down beside Soren and begins to mop up the spill with his own shirt. They clean it up. They sit up. Billy looks at Soren very gently.)*
BILLY. Tomorrow morning? You gonna be here? ... Forever? *(They hold each other's gaze. Billy reaches out to him. Soren doesn't flinch. Lights fade out.)*

End of Play

PROPERTY LIST

Two glasses of water (SHIRLEY)
Ring (BILLY)
Cigarettes, lighter (BILLY)
Box (SOREN)
Tuna fish, can opener (SOREN)
Saucer of milk (SOREN)
Glass of water (BILLY)
Duct tape (BILLY)
Two cups of coffee (SHIRLEY)
Sponge, paper towels (SOREN)
Napkins (BILLY)
Vacuum and attachments (BILLY)
Purse (SHIRLEY)
Laundry (SHIRLEY)
Sofa pillows (SOREN)
Keys (BILLY)
Phone (SHIRLEY)
Composition book, paper (SOREN)
Boxes, hammer (SOREN)
Bags of groceries (BILLY, SHIRLEY)
Book (BILLY)
Clipboard (BILLY)
Pots and pans (BILLY)
Brochures (BILLY)
Newspaper (BILLY)
Leather bag full of plastic toys (SOREN)
Duct tape (SOREN)
Plates of food (SHIRLEY)
Vacuum (SHIRLEY)
Backpack, tool kit (SOREN)
Coke bottle (SOREN)
Boxes (SHIRLEY)
Duct tape (SHIRLEY)
Glass (SOREN)

SOUND EFFECTS

Kitten mewing
Running water
Truck motor
Truck motor stalling
Truck leaving
Vacuum cleaner
Country music
Door slam
Clutch popping
Giggling

NEW PLAYS

★ **THE GREAT AMERICAN TRAILER PARK MUSICAL music and lyrics by David Nehls, book by Betsy Kelso.** Pippi, a stripper on the run, has just moved into Armadillo Acres, wreaking havoc among the tenants of Florida's most exclusive trailer park. "Adultery, strippers, murderous ex-boyfriends, Costco and the Ice Capades. Undeniable fun." –*NY Post.* "Joyful and unashamedly vulgar." –*The New Yorker.* "Sparkles with treasure." –*New York Sun.* [2M, 5W] ISBN: 978-0-8222-2137-1

★ **MATCH by Stephen Belber.** When a young Seattle couple meet a prominent New York choreographer, they are led on a fraught journey that will change their lives forever. "Uproariously funny, deeply moving, enthralling theatre." –*NY Daily News.* "Prolific laughs and ear-to-ear smiles." –*NY Magazine.* [2M, 1W] ISBN: 978-0-8222-2020-6

★ **MR. MARMALADE by Noah Haidle.** Four-year-old Lucy's imaginary friend, Mr. Marmalade, doesn't have much time for her—not to mention he has a cocaine addiction and a penchant for pornography. "Alternately hilarious and heartbreaking." –*The New Yorker.* "A mature and accomplished play." –*LA Times.* "Scathingly observant comedy." –*Miami Herald.* [4M, 2W] ISBN: 978-0-8222-2142-5

★ **MOONLIGHT AND MAGNOLIAS by Ron Hutchinson.** Three men cloister themselves as they work tirelessly to reshape a screenplay that's just not working—*Gone with the Wind.* "Consumers of vintage Hollywood insider stories will eat up Hutchinson's diverting conjecture." –*Variety.* "A lot of fun." –*NY Post.* "A Hollywood dream-factory farce." –*Chicago Sun-Times.* [3M, 1W] ISBN: 978-0-8222-2084-8

★ **THE LEARNED LADIES OF PARK AVENUE by David Grimm, translated and freely adapted from Molière's *Les Femmes Savantes*.** Dicky wants to marry Betty, but her mother's plan is for Betty to wed a most pompous man. "A brave, brainy and barmy revision." –*Hartford Courant.* "A rare but welcome bird in contemporary theatre." –*New Haven Register.* "Roll over Cole Porter." –*Boston Globe.* [5M, 5W] ISBN: 978-0-8222-2135-7

★ **REGRETS ONLY by Paul Rudnick.** A sparkling comedy of Manhattan manners that explores the latest topics in marriage, friendships and squandered riches. "One of the funniest quip-meisters on the planet." –*NY Times.* "Precious moments of hilarity. Devastatingly accurate political and social satire." –*BackStage.* "Great fun." –*CurtainUp.* [3M, 3W] ISBN: 978-0-8222-2223-1

DRAMATISTS PLAY SERVICE, INC.
440 Park Avenue South, New York, NY 10016 212-683-8960 Fax 212-213-1539
postmaster@dramatists.com   www.dramatists.com

NEW PLAYS

★ **AFTER ASHLEY by Gina Gionfriddo.** A teenager is unwillingly thrust into the national spotlight when a family tragedy becomes talk-show fodder. "A work that virtually any audience would find accessible." *–NY Times.* "Deft characterization and caustic humor." *–NY Sun.* "A smart satirical drama." *–Variety.* [4M, 2W] ISBN: 978-0-8222-2099-2

★ **THE RUBY SUNRISE by Rinne Groff.** Twenty-five years after Ruby struggles to realize her dream of inventing the first television, her daughter faces similar battles of faith as she works to get Ruby's story told on network TV. "Measured and intelligent, optimistic yet clear-eyed." *–NY Magazine.* "Maintains an exciting sense of ingenuity." *–Village Voice.* "Sinuous theatrical flair." *–Broadway.com.* [3M, 4W] ISBN: 978-0-8222-2140-1

★ **MY NAME IS RACHEL CORRIE taken from the writings of Rachel Corrie, edited by Alan Rickman and Katharine Viner.** This solo piece tells the story of Rachel Corrie who was killed in Gaza by an Israeli bulldozer set to demolish a Palestinian home. "Heartbreaking urgency. An invigoratingly detailed portrait of a passionate idealist." *–NY Times.* "Deeply authentically human." *–USA Today.* "A stunning dramatization." *–CurtainUp.* [1W] ISBN: 978-0-8222-2222-4

★ **ALMOST, MAINE by John Cariani.** This charming midwinter night's dream of a play turns romantic clichés on their ear as it chronicles the painfully hilarious amorous adventures (and misadventures) of residents of a remote northern town that doesn't quite exist. "A whimsical approach to the joys and perils of romance." *–NY Times.* "Sweet, poignant and witty." *–NY Daily News.* "Aims for the heart by way of the funny bone." *–Star-Ledger.* [2M, 2W] ISBN: 978-0-8222-2156-2

★ **Mitch Albom's TUESDAYS WITH MORRIE by Jeffrey Hatcher and Mitch Albom, based on the book by Mitch Albom.** The true story of Brandeis University professor Morrie Schwartz and his relationship with his student Mitch Albom. "A touching, life-affirming, deeply emotional drama." *–NY Daily News.* "You'll laugh. You'll cry." *–Variety.* "Moving and powerful." *–NY Post.* [2M] ISBN: 978-0-8222-2188-3

★ **DOG SEES GOD: CONFESSIONS OF A TEENAGE BLOCKHEAD by Bert V. Royal.** An abused pianist and a pyromaniac ex-girlfriend contribute to the teen-angst of America's most hapless kid. "A welcome antidote to the notion that the *Peanuts* gang provides merely American cuteness." *–NY Times.* "Hysterically funny." *–NY Post.* "The *Peanuts* kids have finally come out of their shells." *–Time Out.* [4M, 4W] ISBN: 978-0-8222-2152-4

DRAMATISTS PLAY SERVICE, INC.
440 Park Avenue South, New York, NY 10016   212-683-8960   Fax 212-213-1539
postmaster@dramatists.com   www.dramatists.com

NEW PLAYS

★ **RABBIT HOLE by David Lindsay-Abaire.** Winner of the 2007 Pulitzer Prize. Becca and Howie Corbett have everything a couple could want until a life-shattering accident turns their world upside down. "An intensely emotional examination of grief, laced with wit." –*Variety.* "A transcendent and deeply affecting new play." –*Entertainment Weekly.* "Painstakingly beautiful." –*BackStage.* [2M, 3W] ISBN: 978-0-8222-2154-8

★ **DOUBT, A Parable by John Patrick Shanley.** Winner of the 2005 Pulitzer Prize and Tony Award. Sister Aloysius, a Bronx school principal, takes matters into her own hands when she suspects the young Father Flynn of improper relations with one of the male students. "All the elements come invigoratingly together like clockwork." –*Variety.* "Passionate, exquisite, important, engrossing." –*NY Newsday.* [1M, 3W] ISBN: 978-0-8222-2219-4

★ **THE PILLOWMAN by Martin McDonagh.** In an unnamed totalitarian state, an author of horrific children's stories discovers that someone has been making his stories come true. "A blindingly bright black comedy." –*NY Times.* "McDonagh's least forgiving, bravest play." –*Variety.* "Thoroughly startling and genuinely intimidating." –*Chicago Tribune.* [4M, 5 bit parts (2M, 1W, 1 boy, 1 girl)] ISBN: 978-0-8222-2100-5

★ **GREY GARDENS book by Doug Wright, music by Scott Frankel, lyrics by Michael Korie.** The hilarious and heartbreaking story of Big Edie and Little Edie Bouvier Beale, the eccentric aunt and cousin of Jacqueline Kennedy Onassis, once bright names on the social register who became East Hampton's most notorious recluses. "An experience no passionate theatergoer should miss." –*NY Times.* "A unique and unmissable musical." –*Rolling Stone.* [4M, 3W, 2 girls] ISBN: 978-0-8222-2181-4

★ **THE LITTLE DOG LAUGHED by Douglas Carter Beane.** Mitchell Green could make it big as the hot new leading man in Hollywood if Diane, his agent, could just keep him in the closet. "Devastatingly funny." –*NY Times.* "An out-and-out delight." –*NY Daily News.* "Full of wit and wisdom." –*NY Post.* [2M, 2W] ISBN: 978-0-8222-2226-2

★ **SHINING CITY by Conor McPherson.** A guilt-ridden man reaches out to a therapist after seeing the ghost of his recently deceased wife. "Haunting, inspired and glorious." –*NY Times.* "Simply breathtaking and astonishing." –*Time Out.* "A thoughtful, artful, absorbing new drama." –*Star-Ledger.* [3M, 1W] ISBN: 978-0-8222-2187-6

DRAMATISTS PLAY SERVICE, INC.
440 Park Avenue South, New York, NY 10016   212-683-8960   Fax 212-213-1539
postmaster@dramatists.com   www.dramatists.com